Cancer's Lesson on What Truly Matters

CLEARING THE CLUTTER

Personal Stories of Healing, Reflection, and Rediscovery

THROY CAMPBELL

LUCIDBOOKS

Clearing the Clutter: Cancer's Lesson on What Truly Matters
Personal Stories of Healing, Reflection, and Rediscovery
Copyright © 2025 by Throy Campbell

Published by Lucid Books in Houston, TX
www.LucidBooks.com

All rights reserved. No part of this publication may be reproduced, stored in a retrieval system, or transmitted in any form by any means, electronic, mechanical, photocopy, recording, or otherwise, without the prior permission of the publisher, except as provided for by USA copyright law.

eISBN: 978-1-63296-774-9
ISBN: 978-1-63296-773-2

Special Sales: Most Lucid Books titles are available in special quantity discounts. Custom imprinting or excerpting can also be done to fit special needs. Contact Lucid Books at Info@LucidBooks.com

To the courageous individuals who shared their journeys,

This book is for you—the warriors who faced the formidable challenge of cancer with grace, strength, and resilience. It is also for the caregivers, family members, and friends who stood steadfastly by your side, offering love, support, and hope when needed.

Your collective bravery, compassion, and unwavering determination have illuminated the path for others navigating their own battles. Through your shared experiences, you have become beacons of light, reminding us of the strength of the human spirit and the power of community.

Thank you for your trust, honesty, and courage. It is an honor to share your stories with the world.

With deepest gratitude and respect,

Throy Campbell

PREFACE

In life, we often encounter stories that leave an indelible mark on our hearts and minds. This book is a collection of such stories shared by courageous individuals who have faced the formidable challenge of cancer. As the host of the Health Stories Podcast, I have had the profound privilege of engaging in open and heartfelt conversations with these remarkable guests. Their willingness to share their health journeys and encounters with cancer has imparted invaluable life lessons to me.

I approach this book from a unique vantage point. Having never experienced a serious, life-threatening illness myself, I am able to present these stories from an unbiased perspective. This allows me to honor the authenticity of each narrative and ensure that the voices of those who have lived through these experiences are heard loud and clear.

The stories in this book are presented in the first person, giving readers the opportunity to reflect on them through their lenses. This narrative style invites you to walk alongside each storyteller, feeling their triumphs, struggles, and moments of profound insight.

Following each story, I introduce the concept of spiritual decluttering—a practice that encourages us to clear away the mental and emotional clutter that can hinder our well-being. By applying these propositions to each narrative, we gain a deeper understanding of the spiritual and emotional dimensions of the cancer journey.

The main takeaways from these stories are distilled into practical lessons for cancer survivors, offering guidance and inspiration as they navigate their own paths. However, this book is not solely for those touched by cancer. It is a resource for anyone facing illness or life's myriad challenges, providing wisdom and solace in times of need.

I am deeply grateful to the brave individuals who have shared their stories with me. Their resilience and courage are testaments to the strength of the human spirit. I hope this book will serve as a beacon of hope and comfort for all who read it.

With gratitude,

Throy Campbell, PhD

TABLE OF CONTENTS

Preface	v
Foreword	ix
Introduction: Decluttering Life's Stories	1
Against All Odds: A Life of Faith, Hope, and Healing	9
Finding Joy in My Journey: My Battle with Cancer	17
Scars of Strength: My Path to Nursing and Overcoming Cancer	27
Turning Points: My Path from Health to Healing	37
A Journey of Faith and Awareness: Overcoming Prostate Cancer	47
A Path of Purpose: From Zambia to Battling Cancer	57
From Jamaica to NIH: My Unyielding Journey	67
A New Beginning: My Story of Strength and Recovery	77
Faith and Fortitude: Navigating Life's Unexpected Turns	85
Resilient in the Storm: A Journey of Faith, Strength, and Hope	93
From Diagnosis to Determination: My Journey of Survival	101
Navigating Life's Storms: From Childhood Struggles to Cancer Survival	111
Victory is Mine: A Test of Faith, Love, and Strength	121
Silent Warrior: A Journey from Survival to Advocacy	133

Choosing Life: A Journey of Faith and Resilience	141
A Nurse's Journey: Advocacy, Care, and the Fight Against Cancer	149
Spiritual Decluttering Through the Art of Storytelling	155
Developing a Framework	159
Spiritual Decluttering Worksheet	165
Contacting the Author for Seminars, Conferences, and Lectures	175
Endnotes	176

FOREWORD

I met Dr. Campbell when I was in a deep search for answers regarding cancer and God's involvement in the healing process. I saw the carnage of cancer hit too close for comfort. Cancer is so invasive and impactful that even the survivors are always uncertain, waiting for the next test or scan results; I was looking for a tangible solution to offer my parishioners, family, and friends, even myself. While looking for something more than what I was already doing as a pastor, I must confess, that Dr. Campbell came into my ministry, my life, as an answered prayer, as a friend.

Not soon after our friendship started, I noticed he and I shared this deep passion for curbing the emotional and mental impact of cancer and really any other illness in our community, from a spiritual perspective. While I was looking for a Moses-like divine healing intervention, Throy proposed a brilliant and unique practice that consists of inviting individuals not only to tell their stories but also to go through an amazing process and practice of spiritual decluttering, by removing all the emotional and mental clutter that paralyzes the soul from experiencing a wholistic divine intervention.

This practice assists the storytellers in realizing the metanarrative of their stories: God, the Recordkeeper, the Judge, the Waymaker, the sacrificial Lamb Provider, the Ultimate Certainty, and the Guarantor of our future. The book you are about to read, *Clearing the Clutter: Cancer's Lesson on What Truly Matters,* is not a compilation of grim and sad stories of defeat and heartbreak but of glowing victories in the face of uncertainty and chaos; stories by amazing overcomers, courageous ongoing fighters who have and are still experiencing divine grace on their path. These stories help you to witness the practicality of this spiritual decluttering practice in real-life events, with real people, with real pain, and with real longing for complete healing. It does not claim to undo the coping mechanisms one may have or undermine the medical aspects of their treatment. The book does not cast any shadow of guilt to trick you into creating another burden on the soul, a spiritual trauma; but au contraire, it simply opens your eyes to a new reality, a spiritual dimension that has been with us all along.

This outstanding work is born from a genuine sense of empathy and hope, a remarkable professionalism, and a profound spiritual approach to healing. I can attest that you will find it to be an inspiring and practical companion and a workbook for you or a loved one facing cancer. The book is crafted with such unique simplicity and flexibility readers can tailor decluttering practice to their situation.

For all these features and virtues contained in this book- and in addition to what readers will unearth for themselves- I am confident and pleased to recommend it to students of faith in churches, and to spiritual leaders, like me who have always known the importance of the spiritual dimension of healing, but especially the one still in the trench of survival battle against cancer, the family or relative that are witnessing the cancer journey of a loved one.

FOREWORD

I have written these words because I have learned by experience that Throy Campbell's view of decluttering opens the spiritual dimension of your healing when fully embraced in a tenderhearted and humble way.

Roger Wazoua, M-Div
Senior Pastor
Mansfield Seventh Day Adventist Church

INTRODUCTION:
DECLUTTERING LIFE'S STORIES

When faced with uncertainty, decluttering allows us to reflect on our past, gain perspective on the present, and hope for the future.

Imagine gripping a slipping rock at the edge of a tall cliff to save your life. What flashes through your mind—your past, present, or future? At that moment, does it matter how accurately your life story was told? Instead, it's the uncertainty of what lies ahead that takes precedence. Such clarity is often found in life-threatening situations where we are forced to confront what truly matters. Perhaps illness brings this clarity. Perhaps life itself, with all its uncertainties, does the same.

My story began in rural Jamaica, where I grew up in a conservative community rich in religious tradition. From an early age, I was taught to live morally, viewing life as preparation for heaven. I obeyed my elders and was molded by a community that genuinely raised its children.

In the summer of 1989, my community gathered for an evangelistic series. The pastor spoke of Daniel's unwavering faith, even when taken captive in a foreign land. As a young man about to leave home for Munro College, I felt that God was speaking directly to me. Like Daniel, I promised myself that my career would be secured if I remained faithful to God.

The following sermons reinforced my faith as I learned of God's control over the future and the certainty of His kingdom. By the end of the campaign, I was baptized, ready to embark on high school with renewed faith.

At Munro, an all-boys institution, I was introduced to a diverse world. Jamaica's changing society clashed with my conservative upbringing, and I was torn between faith and a more contemporary lifestyle. As my identity formed, I found it easier to relate to celebrities (i.e., music and sports personalities) than to be recognized as a young Christian man.

Later, during my time at the College of Agriculture, Science, and Education, I met my future wife. Our shared religious background helped us navigate life's uncertainties. Our marriage, rooted in faith, was a testament to cultural compatibility.

When we migrated to the United States as a young family, we were thrust into a whirlwind of materialism. The culture shock was overwhelming, and I grappled with questions of identity: Am I a Christian? A father? A student? American society demanded quick adaptation, leaving little time for reflection.

The sudden passing of a fellow international student added another layer to my internal conflict. Life's uncertainties became more apparent, and I struggled to find my footing amidst immigration challenges and financial burdens. Despite these obstacles, my faith remained a constant, reminding me of God's faithfulness.

After earning my master's degree, I encountered a significant setback when I lost my job during the 2010 recession. However, I was blessed with a fellowship that enabled me to return to school, a clear sign that I was not forsaken. Despite this, my physical and mental health deteriorated under the weight of my responsibilities as a husband, father, and student. This challenging period forced me to concentrate on what truly mattered, both mentally and spiritually. I found myself at the edge of a cliff, and instead of holding onto a rock, God held onto me.

SPIRITUAL DECLUTTERING

Reflecting on my journey has deepened my understanding of the importance of decluttering one's life in a spiritual context. I have considered the theories of modern science. There is the psychological application of cognitive behavioral therapy, where recognizing one's thoughts and actions is key to changing behavior patterns.[1] The need for self-acceptance, a component of positive psychology and existential therapy, where individuals reconcile their identity within a larger existential context. The principle of self-compassion also comes to mind, encouraging individuals to forgive their perceived failures and fostering a mindset of gratitude and healing. Additionally, Viktor Frankl's concept of logotherapy suggests that finding meaning even in suffering can transform one's outlook on life and mortality.[2]

My personal experience has led me to the idea of decluttering. This is a deeply personal process, especially in times of uncertainty. It is a mental exercise that helps us evaluate our life's story and determine what is essential—whether it be family, friends, or significant life events. When faced with uncertainty, decluttering allows us to reflect on our past, gain perspective on the present, and hope for the future.

For many, decluttering is also a spiritual practice. Spirituality provides a compass that guides us toward what truly matters. In times of illness, this introspection offers clarity and purpose, helping us prioritize what is most important.

Throughout history, spirituality and healthcare have intertwined. Healers have used rituals, prayers, and herbal remedies to address physical and spiritual needs. Today, this holistic approach is still evident in compassionate, ethical patient care.

Many Christians believe that God is not only the ultimate healer—the Great Physician—but also has the most accurate account of our lives, including our failures and mistakes. This belief offers comfort to those facing life-threatening situations. The certainty of God's mercy and grace provides clarity and hope, even in the most desperate circumstances. By decluttering spiritually, believers can find peace in their faith, trusting that God's grace will prevail even in grave illness.

DECLUTTERING AND CANCER SURVIVORS

While I haven't had a life-threatening illness, the stories of close friends and family members as cancer survivors have sharpened my perspective on the concept of spiritual decluttering. Furthermore, as a research scientist in clinical settings, I have realized the limitations of science in healing the whole person.

Cancer can be profoundly grave, marked by intense physical, emotional, and spiritual challenges. It often involves a journey through pain, uncertainty, and fear as individuals confront their mortality and the impact of the disease on their lives and loved ones. The gravity of a cancer story lies not only in the medical battles fought but also in the deep emotional scars and the relentless struggle for hope and resilience. Each story is a testament to one's capacity to endure and find meaning amidst the darkest times.

Understanding one's life story in a spiritual context allows survivors to declutter and view their struggles and triumphs through a lens of faith and God's divine mercy, creating a sense of security—not by human standards but through God's divine providence.

The Bible teaches that God keeps accurate records of our lives. Cancer survivors can take comfort in knowing that God sees their whole story, not just the pain or failures, but the endurance and faith. His records serve not to condemn us but to showcase His mercy and compassion. Most importantly, God sees the context and environment in which one was born. It is not about one's ability to control outcomes but accepting God's grace, which guides us through every stage of life.

Decluttering is a reflective process where we properly frame life's trials and victories and realize that every step taken was recorded by God—not for judgment, but as a testament to His unfailing love and mercy. Each story is a narrative of grace, showing how faith can illuminate the darkest of times and how God's divine record-keeping offers hope in the knowledge that their lives are deeply valued and eternally remembered.

STEPS OF SPIRITUAL DECLUTTERING

The following steps are not necessarily progressive but can be iterative:

1. **Recognize Divine Record-Keeping:** Understand that it is God, not humans, who keeps an accurate record of all our thoughts and actions, both good and bad.
2. **Embrace God's Perspective:** Accept that God has a universal understanding of your human nature and the societal context in which you were born and raised.
3. **Heavenly Judgment:** Know that God's records of our lives are intended for a heavenly court, not a human one.
4. **Accept Divine Sacrifice:** Embrace God's substitutionary death and His willingness to reward you if you accept Him as your Savior.
5. **Acknowledge and Reject Wrongdoings:** Accept your wrongdoings that partly led to God's sacrifice on the cross and reject this undesired version of yourself.
6. **Reconciliation in Christ:** Accept that you are reconciled in Christ.
7. **Certainty of Eternal Life:** Accept the certainty of eternal life and see the positive outcome of life's challenges, including a terminal illness.

APPLYING SPIRITUAL DECLUTTERING

Spiritual decluttering is beneficial at any stage of life but can be particularly powerful during illness. A life-threatening condition forces us to confront our mortality, stripping away the unnecessary and revealing what is most essential.

Through open conversations with cancer survivors, I have learned invaluable lessons. These stories have profoundly impacted me with an unbiased perspective. I hope they will resonate with readers and encourage them to declutter their own lives, seeking clarity and purpose in the face of uncertainty.

CLEARING THE CLUTTER

REFLECTIONS

AGAINST ALL ODDS: A LIFE OF FAITH, HOPE, AND HEALING

By Tracia Williams

My journey isn't over yet, and I will continue to fight with every ounce of strength I have.

I was born on January 16, 1986, with spina bifida—a condition that meant I faced challenges from the moment I took my first breath. I was supposed to arrive on Valentine's Day, but I guess I couldn't wait to make my entrance into this world. My mother, who had just celebrated her birthday with her coworkers the day before, went into labor unexpectedly. My father, working in a different department at the hospital, heard the announcement over the intercom: "Mr. Franklin, your wife is in labor." And so, I made my early appearance, already bringing my parents closer in the face of adversity.

I didn't know it then, but my life was about to be filled with trials that would test my faith and resilience. Right after I was born, I had to be rushed to another hospital to close a hole in my back caused by spina bifida. My mother didn't even get the chance to hold me. I was taken away, leaving my parents in a turbulence of worry and fear. My father, the caring and devoted man he was, drove back and forth between hospitals, his heart torn between his newborn daughter and his wife.

The surgery to close my spine was successful, and after two long weeks, I was finally able to go home. But the relief was short-lived. Not long after we got home, my parents noticed my face had swollen and turned blue. In a panic, they rushed me back to the hospital. I was diagnosed with hydrocephalus, a condition where excess fluid builds up in the brain. I needed emergency brain surgery to place a shunt that would drain the fluid. I was just two weeks old when I had my first brain surgery. My parents must have been terrified, but God's hand was on me, and I recovered well.

Growing up was far from easy. I needed multiple surgeries—on my feet, on my brain—but I never gave up. At the age of five, my shunt malfunctioned, and I had to undergo yet another brain surgery. During the operation, the doctors discovered something miraculous: my brain was functioning just fine without the shunt. That was the first time I truly felt the power of prayer. My parents' faith grew stronger with every surgery, and so did mine.

Doctors had told my parents that I wouldn't be able to walk, think for myself, or even sit up. They painted a grim picture, one that seemed impossible to overcome. But my parents held onto hope and prayed. And when I took my first steps at the age of two, it was as if I was defying all the odds. It was a small victory, but it meant the world to us. My parents' unwavering faith in God became the foundation of my strength.

School wasn't easy either. I walked differently from other kids and was the only Black student in my class. I was often bullied, and it hurt, but I knew I was special. I believed God had made me this way for a reason, and that belief carried me through the tough times.

In 2021, life dealt me another harsh blow. I lost my father to gastric cancer. His passing shattered me. He was my best friend, role model, and biggest supporter. We had a bond that was unbreakable and losing him felt like losing a part of me. I remember praying so hard for his healing, begging God to let him stay. But sometimes, God's plans are different from ours. My father, despite his suffering, never lost his faith. He was like a modern-day Job, holding onto his belief in God's goodness even in the face of unimaginable pain. His strength and faith continue to inspire me to this day.

Just a year after my father passed, I discovered a lump in my left breast. I had a gut feeling it was something serious. Doctors initially dismissed it as a cyst, but I couldn't shake the feeling that something was wrong. After more tests and biopsies, my worst fears were confirmed: I was diagnosed with stage one ductal carcinoma in March 2023. I remember the moment the doctor said the word "cancer." My body shook, my mind went blank, and fear gripped my heart. But deep down, I knew I wasn't alone. God was with me. He had been preparing me for this battle long before it arrived, and He gave me a sense of peace that I can't quite explain.

Since then, I've undergone a double mastectomy and several rounds of chemotherapy. I've faced treatments, blood clots, and surgeries that seemed endless. There were days when I didn't know if I could keep going, but I did. My church family has been my anchor, lifting me up in prayer and love. Even when I had to postpone brain surgery for Chiari Malformation Type II because of my cancer treatments, I never lost hope. My faith has been my guiding light through the darkest of times.

God is the source of my strength. I've been through so much, but I've never questioned His plan for me. I refuse to let fear consume me. I know my journey isn't over yet, and I will continue to fight with every ounce of strength I have. When I come out of this, there won't even be the smell of smoke on me—just like Shadrach, Meshach, and Abednego in the fiery furnace. I'm holding onto God's promises, and I know He isn't done with me yet.

Every challenge I've faced has shaped me, but they don't define me. I am a daughter of the Most High, and I trust that He will continue to guide me through this journey. My story is still being written, and I believe with all my heart that miracles happen every day.

DECLUTTERING

1. **Recognize Divine Record-Keeping**

Tracia consistently acknowledges that God is the keeper of her life's record. From her birth with spina bifida to her ongoing cancer battle, she reflects on the idea that God is aware of every hardship, success, and even the moments of despair. She frequently refers to God's role in guiding her, suggesting her belief in divine record-keeping. This recognition allows her to find peace and understanding, knowing that a higher power accounts for all her struggles.

2. **Embrace God's Perspective**

Tracia's story shows her acceptance of God's perspective, especially in the face of overwhelming health challenges. She reflects that her life's difficulties, from childhood surgeries to her father's death and her cancer diagnosis, are all part of God's greater plan. This belief helps her trust in God's understanding of her struggles, even when doctors told (her parents) she wouldn't walk or when she feared the worst after discovering her breast cancer. She perceives her suffering as part of the human condition, yet one where God's love prevails.

3. **Heavenly Judgment**

In her story, Tracia rejects the idea that her suffering is a punishment from God. Instead, she views the challenges she faces as part of the spiritual journey meant to prepare her for eternal life. She does not worry about judgment from others but remains focused on living according to God's will, knowing that her trials will be judged in heaven, not by human standards.

4. **Accept Divine Sacrifice**

Tracia frequently speaks of God's sacrifice and her reliance on Him. She references the belief that Christ's death on the cross paved the way for her to receive peace and eternal life, even amid her suffering. This belief enables her to find comfort during her struggles, knowing that the sacrifice made for her allows her to endure with hope and assurance that her hardships are not in vain.

5. Acknowledge and Reject Wrongdoings

Though Tracia does not dwell on specific wrongdoings, she does acknowledge the spiritual warfare she endures, especially when she speaks of the devil planting seeds of doubt and fear in her mind. She recognizes moments when she feels overwhelmed by fear but rejects those feelings, aligning herself with God's peace. This indicates her acknowledgment of human weakness and her decision to reject negativity and temptation.

6. Reconciliation in Christ

Reconciliation is central to Tracia's narrative. She speaks about her strong connection with God and how, through her faith, she reconciles her pain and suffering. By viewing her cancer and other struggles as part of a larger divine plan, she is able to accept her circumstances without resentment. Her relationship with Christ reassures her that she is cared for and loved, regardless of the challenges she faces.

7. Certainty of Eternal Life

Tracia's faith in eternal life is unwavering. She views her journey as one that will ultimately lead to spiritual victory. Her belief that God will see her through each trial and that there is a place for her beyond this life fuels her ability to endure even the most difficult moments. This certainty of eternal life gives her peace and confidence in God's plan, allowing her to view each day as a step closer to spiritual fulfillment.

Major Takeaways for Cancer Survivors:
1. **Faith as a Foundation:** Spirituality can provide strength, peace, and hope during difficult times.
2. **Support Systems Matter:** A strong, faith-based support system is crucial for enduring treatments and surgeries.
3. **Resilience in the Face of Fear:** Reject despair and hold onto hope by trusting in a higher plan.
4. **Spiritual Growth:** Challenges can foster a deeper connection with one's faith.
5. **Eternal Perspective:** Viewing cancer as part of a spiritual journey can lead to greater fulfillment and strength.

CLEARING THE CLUTTER

REFLECTIONS

FINDING JOY IN MY JOURNEY:
MY BATTLE WITH CANCER

By Stacey Edwards

We can all find something to be grateful for, even in the darkest times. For me, it was the little things.

My name is Stacey Edwards, and my life has been a tapestry of roles—I'm a nurse, a mother, a wife, and a friend. However, the roles I never asked for have shaped me the most: cancer patient and survivor. Over the past seven years, I've faced cancer three times. It hasn't been an easy journey, but through it all, I've found joy, leaned on my faith, and embraced the love and support of those around me. This is my story of resilience.

It all began in 2017. I was out with my daughter on a sunny afternoon, enjoying a simple day together at the mall, when I felt a sharp, stabbing pain in my breast. It was as if someone had jabbed me, but no one was there. The pain lingered, a silent warning I couldn't ignore. As a nurse, I had seen my fair share of medical issues, but nothing could have prepared me for the moment when I was told those life-changing words: "You have breast cancer." I felt my world tilt, my breath caught in my chest, and in that instant, everything changed.

When the call came, I was home alone. My husband, Dean, who usually isn't home during the day, walked through the door just as I received the news. Isn't it funny how life works sometimes? It felt like a divine intervention as if God knew I needed Dean's arms around me at that very moment. My heart broke, and I crumbled into his embrace, the weight of the diagnosis crashing down on us both. The journey that followed was a stormy path of fear and endless hospital visits—surgery, six grueling rounds of chemotherapy, and the emotional and physical challenges that come with it. Each day felt like an uphill battle, but I kept reminding myself, "Each day is an opportunity," and I clung to that mantra like a lifeline.

Breaking the news to our children, Jonathan and Jadyn, was one of the hardest things I've ever had to do. They were just ten and eleven—so young, so innocent. I didn't want to burden them with worry, but they needed to know. I tried to be strong, to reassure them that Mommy would be okay, but inside, I was terrified. When I lost my hair, I thought it would scare them, but Jonathan looked at me with his sweet, earnest eyes and said, "Mommy, we love you with or without hair." That simple, profound statement was like a balm to my soul. Their love and unwavering belief in me gave me the strength to keep going, even on the darkest days.

Five years passed, and I was so close to that elusive milestone—being considered cancer-free. We had begun to breathe a little easier, to imagine a future beyond cancer. But just as I was about to reach that milestone, I noticed something wasn't right. I hadn't had a period in years, but suddenly, I was bleeding. A sense of dread filled me as I made an appointment with my doctor. When the news came that it was uterine cancer, I felt like I had been punched in the gut. I told myself, "You're not gonna cry, girl. You're not gonna cry." But the tears came anyway, an uncontrollable flood of fear and frustration. It felt like my body was betraying me all over again.

The second diagnosis was like a cruel twist of fate, but I knew I had to fight again. There was no other choice. Another surgery, more chemo—this time, I knew what to expect, but that didn't make it any easier. I decided then and there that I would find joy in this journey, no matter how difficult. I believe we can all find something to be grateful for, even in the darkest times. For me, it was the little things—the warmth of my children's hugs, the gentle strength of my husband's hand in mine, the unwavering support of my friends. My church community became my lifeline, lifting me up with their prayers and encouragement when I felt like I couldn't go on.

Just as I thought I was finally in the clear, the cancer returned for a third time in 2023. This time, it had spread to my lymph nodes. I can't even begin to describe how it felt to hear that news again. It shook me to my core in a way that the previous diagnoses hadn't. I had never asked, "Why me?" with the first two diagnoses, but this time, I couldn't help it. I was scared, exhausted, and overwhelmed. It felt like life had dealt me one blow too many. But giving up was never an option for me. I chose to fight, even though the treatment hit me harder than ever before.

Dean has been my rock through all of this. He's the calm, rational one, always keeping me grounded when I start to feel like I'm losing it. He doesn't share his worries with me—he knows I have enough of my own—but I can see the pain in his eyes. He hurts for me, for our children, for all we've had to endure. Yet, he's always there, reminding me of the good in our lives, even when I don't want to hear it. His love has been my anchor, steadying me when the storm inside my heart rages out of control.

Jonathan and Jadyn have grown up watching me fight this battle. Jadyn is my emotional one, always ready to talk or cry when the news is bad. Jonathan, on the other hand, keeps his feelings to himself. He's so strong, always there to hold my hand or rub my feet when the pain is too much. I wish I knew what was going on in his mind, but he doesn't share. I can only hope that he's coping as well as he seems to be. My heart aches for what they've had to witness, for the childhood innocence cancer has stolen from them.

There are days when loneliness creeps in, especially when the house is empty and I'm left alone with my thoughts and the pain. But I refuse to let those moments define me. I push myself to go to work and church and to stay connected with people. It's my way of holding onto some sense of normalcy. My friends have been incredible, showing up in ways I never expected. From care packages to simple text messages, their love and support have meant the world to me. I've learned that I'm never truly alone.

One of the things that has helped me through this third battle is my "lucky" jean jacket. It started as a small thing—just a few pins that I thought would make me feel good during treatments. But after I posted about it on Facebook, friends began sending me pins so they could be with me in spirit. Now, my jacket is covered in pins, each one representing someone who is walking this journey with me. It's a tangible reminder that even when I'm sitting in that chemo chair by myself, I'm surrounded by love.

This journey has taught me so much about life, resilience, and the importance of being intentional in our actions. If there's one thing I've learned, it's that you have to want it for yourself. Whether you're fighting cancer or just getting through a tough day, you have to find that "it" factor within you. Life isn't always easy, but it's still my life, and I will make the most of it while I'm here.

I know I've been through more than most, but I also know that I'm not alone. My family, friends, and faith keep me going, and I am eternally grateful for that. I choose to find joy in the journey, love deeply, and live fully. That's my story, and I hope it inspires others to keep fighting, no matter what life throws at them.

DECLUTTERING

1. **Recognize Divine Record-Keeping**

Stacey's journey is a testament to her deep faith in God and her belief that her life's story is not just her own but is also being watched over by a higher power. Throughout her battles with cancer, she frequently mentions seeing God's hand in her life, from her husband miraculously being there when she received her first diagnosis to the timely interventions that allowed her to continue her treatments. She recognizes that her thoughts, actions, and the unfolding events of her life are all part of a divine record carefully noted by God.

2. Embrace God's Perspective

Stacey embraces the idea that God understands the complexities of her life and the societal context in which she was raised. She acknowledges that her journey, filled with trials and pain, is part of a broader divine plan that she may not fully understand but trusts, nonetheless. Her ability to find joy in the journey and remain hopeful despite multiple cancer diagnoses reflects her acceptance of God's greater perspective on her life.

3. Heavenly Judgment

Stacey's focus is not on the judgment of others but on living a life that aligns with her faith and values. She recognizes that her life's true record will be evaluated in a heavenly court, where God's understanding and mercy prevail. This understanding allows her to live authentically and courageously, knowing that her life's challenges and her responses to them are seen and understood by God.

4. Accept Divine Sacrifice

Stacey's faith in Christ and His sacrifice is a cornerstone of her strength. She acknowledges the importance of accepting Christ as her Savior, which gives her the hope of being rewarded in the afterlife. This belief helps her to find peace, even in the face of terminal illness, knowing that her suffering is temporary and that she is reconciled with God through Christ.

5. Acknowledge and Reject Wrongdoings

While Stacey's story does not explicitly delve into personal wrongdoings, her journey reflects a broader rejection of despair and hopelessness. She acknowledges the reality of her situation but rejects the notion that it defines her. Instead, she chooses to live a life filled with gratitude, love, and resilience.

6. Reconciliation in Christ

Stacey's reconciliation with God through Christ is evident in her peace and acceptance of her circumstances. She finds comfort in her faith, knowing that she is reconciled with God and that her life's journey has a greater purpose, no matter how difficult. Her ability to continue fighting, supported by her faith and community, showcases her belief in this reconciliation.

7. Certainty of Eternal Life

Stacey's certainty of eternal life is a significant aspect of her story. She views her battles with cancer not as an end but as part of a journey that will eventually lead to eternal life. This certainty allows her to face her illness with hope, knowing that her suffering is temporary and that a positive outcome awaits her in the afterlife.

Major Takeaways for Cancer Survivors:

1. **Finding Joy in the Journey:** Focus on positive aspects of life to maintain hope and resilience.
2. **Leaning on Faith and Spirituality:** Faith can provide comfort and strength during tough times.

3. **Building and Relying on a Support System:** A strong support network is crucial for emotional and practical support.
4. **Maintaining a Positive and Resilient Attitude:** Staying positive can significantly improve quality of life.
5. **Acknowledging the Emotional Impact on Family:** Open communication helps families cope with the emotional impact.
6. **Understanding and Accepting Your Own Needs:** Listen to your body and mind and seek help when needed.
7. **Navigating the Healthcare System and Financial Challenges:** Be proactive in understanding treatment plans and financial resources.
8. **Recognizing the Importance of Advocacy and Awareness:** Advocate for yourself and share your story to help others.
9. **Embracing the Uncertainty of Life:** Accept life's uncertainties and find peace in a higher purpose.

MY BATTLE WITH CANCER

REFLECTIONS

SCARS OF STRENGTH:
MY PATH TO NURSING AND OVERCOMING CANCER

By Christy Boucher

The physical changes didn't bother me; in fact,
I embraced them.

My journey into nursing didn't start the way most do. In my 40s, I was entrenched in the world of finance and accounting—a field that provided me with stability and security but left my soul yearning for something more. As a single mother, balancing work, school, and raising my daughter, I often found myself questioning the path I was on. During one of those soul-searching moments, I picked up Rick Warren's The Purpose Driven Life. That book changed everything for me. It made me realize that time is precious, and if I was going to invest in furthering my education, it needed to be in something that truly mattered to me and the world. And so, I took a leap of faith and enrolled in nursing school.

Graduating and stepping into the role of an ER nurse was the most challenging and fulfilling decision I've ever made. People thought I was crazy, leaving behind a well-paying, stable job in my 40s. "Why would you do that?" they asked. But for me, it wasn't about comfort or money—it was about purpose. I wanted to feel that the work I was doing meant something, that it mattered on a fundamental level. Nursing gave me that. I felt alive in a way I never had before.

But just five years into my nursing career, my life took another unexpected turn. I was diagnosed with breast cancer. I remember the moment like it was yesterday. My heart stopped. I could almost hear my mother's voice echoing through the years. She, too, had faced this battle in her 50s. She fought hard, undergoing a lumpectomy and radiation. Although she survived cancer, she later succumbed to heart disease. I always wondered if the radiation had contributed to her health issues later on. So, when my own diagnosis came in 2018, I knew I was standing at a crossroads.

I had a choice to make: a lumpectomy followed by radiation or a double mastectomy. The weight of the decision pressed down on me like a heavy stone. I thought of my mother's journey, of friends who had suffered long after their treatments ended. I spoke with women who had been through radiation and heard their stories of burns, fatigue, and, in some cases, cancer returning. A close friend who had undergone radiation developed lung cancer later on. All these stories swirled in my mind as I tried to find clarity in the chaos.

Ultimately, I chose a double mastectomy. It was more than just a medical decision—it was a choice for peace of mind. I didn't want to live with the constant fear of cancer returning or the possibility of facing the harsh side effects of radiation. It was one of the hardest decisions I've ever made, but it felt right for me. Even with all my medical knowledge, nothing could prepare me for the emotional upheaval that came with it. I researched, I talked to doctors, and I leaned on friends and fellow survivors, but in the end, I had to trust my own heart and make the decision that would give me the most peace.

The surgery itself was a grueling experience. I chose to undergo a DIEP flap reconstruction, which meant taking tissue from my abdomen to reconstruct my breasts. It was a complex and life-altering procedure. The physical toll was immense. I have a long scar from hip to hip, a reminder of what I endured. For weeks, I couldn't even stand up straight. I needed help with everything—from showering to getting out of bed. My husband became my rock, my lifeline. He was there, patient and loving, helping me through each painful step of recovery. I never truly realized how interconnected our bodies are until the simplest tasks felt like climbing mountains.

But even through the pain, I found a strange sense of gratitude. The physical changes didn't bother me; in fact, I embraced them. Before the surgery, I had considered a breast reduction, and now I had a flatter stomach and smaller breasts. My scars, as long and jagged as they are, tell the story of my survival. They are a testament to my strength and resilience. My daughter, who was incredibly close to her grandmother, stood by my side every step of the way. She's vigilant about her health now and more aware of the importance of early detection. Together, we carry the legacy of my mother's battle with breast cancer but also the strength and resilience that have become our family's heritage.

It's been nearly six years now, and I'm cancer-free. I look back and feel a deep sense of gratitude. My journey wasn't as grueling as it could have been—I didn't have to endure chemotherapy or radiation. I didn't lose my hair, and I didn't spend months feeling sick. Sometimes, I feel like I didn't suffer "enough" to belong to the community of cancer survivors. But then, a dear friend reminded me: I survived breast cancer. I had the surgery, I endured the recovery, and I'm still here, living my life to the fullest. That's what matters.

As a nurse, I've seen the worst that cancer can do. I've seen patients who didn't have the resources I did, who struggled not just with the disease but with the financial and emotional toll it takes. It's why I'm so passionate about early detection and why I advocate for better patient-provider relationships. When my first surgeon dismissed my concerns with flippant remarks, I realized how crucial it is for healthcare providers to listen and truly hear their patients. We deserve to be heard and be part of the decision-making process. It's our bodies, our lives, our battles.

If there's one thing I want others to take away from my story, it's this: advocate for yourself. Do your research, talk to others, and make the right decision for you. No one else can do that for you. Whether it's cancer or any other health challenge, it's your body, life, and journey. Fight for it. Believe in yourself. And remember, even in the darkest moments, there is always hope. There is always light.

DECLUTTERING

1. **Recognize Divine Record-Keeping**

Christy's decision to shift careers from accounting to nursing represents a pivotal moment where she recognized a deeper calling. Through reading *The Purpose Driven Life*, she became more attuned to the idea that her life had a purpose beyond financial stability and routine work. In this sense, Christy recognized that there is more to life than human accomplishments, aligning with the concept that God is the ultimate keeper of the record of our lives. Her shift toward nursing reflects a recognition of a higher calling, aligning with her values of service and purpose.

2. **Embrace God's Perspective**

Christy's breast cancer diagnosis came with an overwhelming sense of uncertainty. Still, her decision-making process shows that she sought to understand her situation from a perspective larger than her immediate fears. She deeply considered her mother's journey and reflected on her role as a mother, showing that she sought to understand her human experience in a broader, spiritual context. She navigated her uncertainty by looking at the medical facts and how her decisions could impact her future and her family, demonstrating an embrace of a perspective that transcends the present.

3. **Heavenly Judgment**

Throughout her decision-making process regarding her treatment, Christy faced judgment from doctors who questioned her choice to opt for a double mastectomy. She rejected these human judgments and focused on what she felt was best for her long-term health and peace of mind. This mirrors the principle that God's judgment is what ultimately matters, not the judgment of humans. Christy's commitment to choosing what she believed was right for her body reflects a deep understanding that her life choices are hers, aligning with the concept that only God keeps an accurate and divine record of our lives.

4. Accept Divine Sacrifice

While Christy's story doesn't explicitly mention religious sacrifice, her approach to cancer and recovery reflects an acceptance of the sacrifices that life demands, which can be interpreted through a spiritual lens. Her double mastectomy and reconstruction required a deep personal sacrifice, both physically and emotionally. She embraced the idea that through suffering and hardship, she could still emerge with a new, positive outlook, aligning with the spiritual idea of embracing Christ's sacrifice and the transformation that comes with it.

5. Acknowledge and Reject Wrongdoings

Christy's story involves moments where she rejects negative influences. She recognized when her surgeon made flippant remarks about her treatment choices and rejected his approach by finding another doctor who aligned with her values. This represents her rejection of the negative aspects of her experience—the pressure to conform to others' expectations. Spiritually, this can be seen as Christy acknowledging and rejecting the undesired versions of her circumstances, choosing instead to follow her own moral compass, which aligns with her sense of personal integrity and faith in her decisions.

6. **Reconciliation in Christ**

As Christy recovered and reflected on her surgery, she came to terms with the changes in her body and the challenges of her journey. She found peace in her new physical form, expressing satisfaction with the outcome of her surgery, and even saw it as a positive transformation. Her ability to embrace her new body and her scars represents a form of reconciliation, which parallels the spiritual notion of reconciliation in Christ—finding peace and healing after going through a trial.

7. **Certainty of Eternal Life**

Though Christy doesn't explicitly discuss eternal life, her resilience in facing breast cancer and her commitment to advocating for early detection speaks to a belief in a future beyond the immediate challenges of life. She ensures her daughter's health through education about breast cancer, reflecting her belief in the continuity of life beyond her struggles. This mirrors the concept of accepting the certainty of eternal life, as Christy sees the positive outcome of her trials and continues to live with a renewed sense of purpose and hope.

Major Takeaways for Other Cancer Survivors

1. **Advocate for Yourself:** Trust yourself and make informed decisions by seeking multiple perspectives and doing your research.
2. **Don't Let Others' Judgments Influence Your Choices:** Stay true to your values and instincts, even if others, including medical professionals, question your decisions.

3. **The Importance of Emotional Support:** Surround yourself with a strong support system of family, friends, and coworkers who offer encouragement and practical help.
4. **Every Survivor's Journey is Different:** Avoid comparing your experience to others; every cancer journey is unique and valid.
5. **Early Detection is Key:** Regular screenings and self-examinations are crucial as early detection can significantly impact treatment options and outcomes.
6. **Physical Scars Can Be a Source of Pride:** Embrace your post-surgery body and view scars as symbols of strength and survival.
7. **Healing is a Gradual Process:** Understand that both physical and emotional healing takes time, and it's okay to feel vulnerable or unsure.
8. **Get Educated and Use Available Resources:** Proactively educate yourself about treatment options and recovery by using resources like apps and support groups.
9. **Live with Purpose:** Finding and living with purpose can provide strength and motivation, especially during challenging times.

MY PATH TO NURSING AND OVERCOMING CANCER

REFLECTIONS

TURNING POINTS:
MY PATH FROM HEALTH TO HEALING

By Chris Knight

You have to let us wash your feet, brother.

Everything seemed perfect. It was New Year's Eve 2018, and life couldn't have been better. I was 40 years old, a devoted husband to Lindsey, and a proud father of three. We had a routine that worked, a home filled with love, and a life that was, in every sense, fulfilling. Thanks to eight years of Brazilian Jiu-Jitsu, I was in the best shape of my life. I was eating right, training hard, and felt like I could take on anything that came my way.

But life has a way of changing everything in a heartbeat. New Year's Day 2019 arrived, and with it, a shadow that would alter my world forever. The night before had been filled with laughter and celebration at a friend's house, ringing in the new year with the people we cared about. But when I woke up that morning, I felt drained, as if all my energy had been siphoned away. It wasn't the usual post-party fatigue; something deeper was wrong. Determined to shake it off, I went to our usual New Year's Day open mat session at the Jiu-Jitsu gym, hoping a good workout would clear my head.

Normally, I could spar for 30 minutes without breaking a sweat. But that day, I couldn't last more than a few seconds without feeling completely wiped out. My heart pounded in my chest, and I struggled to catch my breath. It was like my body was fighting against me, refusing to cooperate. I told myself I must have overdone it the night before or was coming down with something minor. But as days turned into weeks, the exhaustion grew worse. It wrapped around me like a heavy blanket I couldn't shake off.

I finally called a friend who was an orthopedic surgeon, thinking maybe I had injured myself, or there was something minor going on. But when the tests came back, the news hit me like a punch to the gut: I had blood clots in my left side, including my jugular. Blood clots? It felt surreal, like something that couldn't possibly happen to me. I was healthy—this wasn't supposed to happen. He suggested I see a hematologist, but before I could even make that appointment, things took a terrifying turn.

One day, while at work, the fatigue and discomfort became unbearable. I decided to head to the emergency room. After a series of tests and a CT scan, the doctor came in with a look that told me everything I needed to know before he spoke. "You have a tumor in your chest," he said gently. They suspected it was lymphoma, a word that felt foreign and terrifying all at once.

I left the hospital in a fog. How could this be happening? Just days ago, I was fine, and now I had cancer? It felt like my whole world had been ripped away from me, leaving nothing but fear and uncertainty in its place. On the drive home, my hands trembled on the steering wheel. How was I going to tell Lindsey? I called her and said we needed to talk when I got home. But she knew something was wrong, and before I could even pull into the driveway, I found myself telling her everything. I heard the shock in her voice, the fear that matched my own. We were blindsided, struggling to grasp this new, terrifying reality.

For a while, we kept the news from our kids. They were still so young, and we didn't want to burden them with the fear that now weighed down every moment of our lives. But Lindsey and I carried the constant, crushing worry with us. I remember lying awake at night, asking myself repeatedly, "Have I been a good husband? A good father? A good friend?" Those questions haunted me more than the diagnosis itself. I thought about all the things I might not see—my kids growing up, growing old with Lindsey, all the life I had yet to live.

The following weeks were a blur of doctor's appointments and tests. I was diagnosed with non-Hodgkin's lymphoma B-cell, a cancer that typically affects older adults. It didn't make sense. I was in the best shape of my life, yet here I was, facing a battle I never saw coming. The doctors laid out a treatment plan, but there were so many unknowns. I had a port installed for chemotherapy, but there was a complication. The tumor in my chest had blocked off access to the usual spot, so they had to place it lower, near my groin. I felt like my body was betraying me, piece by piece.

Then came the day I'll never forget. It was a Thursday, and I thought I was just going in for a routine check-up before starting chemo the following week. But the doctor called me back into his office and told me they had reviewed my pathology again. My cancer was far more aggressive than they had originally thought. Instead of starting chemo on a regular outpatient schedule, they admitted me to the hospital on the spot. I didn't even have a bag packed. I was scared, unprepared, and suddenly staring down at the start of a battle I wasn't ready for.

The chemotherapy was relentless. From Friday to Wednesday, I was in the hospital, receiving treatment around the clock. I'd finish my last bag of chemo on Wednesday evening and be discharged later that night, only to come back again in three weeks. It wasn't just the physical toll—the nausea, the weakness, the sheer exhaustion—it was the mental and emotional weight that threatened to crush me. I felt like I was living in a nightmare, just trying to hold on for the sake of my family.

During this time, the love and support from my friends and family became my lifeline. My next-door neighbor, Randy Rogers, was a friend I'd known since we were three years old. He knew I wasn't going to be able to work during my treatment and saw the financial strain it was putting on us. One day, he came to me and offered to help. But I was too proud, too stubborn. I told him I had it covered and that we'd be fine. But Randy didn't back down. He and another lifelong friend, Lance Brown, visited me in the hospital. Lance brought a painting he'd done of Jesus washing the feet of the apostles. He looked at me and said, "Chris, you have to let us wash your feet, brother."

At that moment, something inside me broke. Lance explained that by refusing help, I was taking away the blessing from others who wanted to support me. I had never thought of it that way before. Accepting help wasn't a sign of weakness—it was allowing others to show their love in the only way they knew how. From that moment on, I realized I needed to let go of my pride, open my heart, and accept the help offered.

As the chemo sessions dragged on, I found myself turning to my faith more than ever before. I had always believed in God, but this experience brought me closer to Him in ways I hadn't expected. I prayed more, studied the Bible, and faced my mortality head-on. I realized how fragile life is and how quickly it can all be taken away. And in that realization, I found a new clarity, a determination to make every day count, to be a better husband, father, and friend. I wanted to live fully because I knew now, more than ever, that tomorrow wasn't promised.

The financial side of cancer was something I couldn't ignore, either. Even with good insurance, the costs were staggering. I remember sitting in the finance office at the hospital, looking at the numbers on the page and thinking, "How do people do this?" One bag of chemo was $15,000, and I needed 36 bags. It was overwhelming. I couldn't help but think of all the people who didn't have the resources we did, who faced this fight not just against cancer but against the crushing financial burden that came with it. That's when the idea for the Guardian Knight Cancer Foundation was born.

After I finished my treatment and began to recover, we launched the foundation. We wanted to help others in the same situation, facing the battle for their lives and the financial strain that comes with it. Through events like golf tournaments, we've raised funds to support over 46 patients, providing financial assistance for treatment costs, living expenses, and whatever they need. But it's more than just money—we build relationships with each patient, offering support and guidance through their journey.

Cancer took so much from me, but it also gave me a new perspective, a deeper faith, and a commitment to help others. I've come out of this stronger, more grateful, more aware of the beauty in the simple things—a sunrise, the laughter of my kids, the love of my wife. I've learned to live each day with purpose, to make every moment count.

I wouldn't wish cancer on anyone, but it taught me more about life, love, and faith than anything else ever could. It brought me closer to the people I care about closer to God and gave me a mission to help others in their time of need. As long as I'm here, I'll keep fighting—not just for myself, but for everyone facing this battle.

DECLUTTERING

1. **Recognize Divine Record-Keeping:**

In Chris's journey, realizing his mortality brought about deep self-reflection. He began to think about his life, questioning whether he had been a good husband, father, and friend. This introspection aligns with the concept of divine record-keeping, where Chris became aware that his thoughts and actions were being "recorded" in a spiritual sense. He recognized that his life was not just about the physical achievements but also about the moral and spiritual legacy he was leaving behind.

2. **Embrace God's Perspective:**
Chris's battle with cancer led him to a deeper connection with his faith. He began to see his situation through a spiritual lens, understanding that God has a greater perspective on his life. This shift in perspective helped Chris to accept his illness as part of a larger divine plan, one that he might not fully understand but trusted, nonetheless. He acknowledged that God's understanding of his life encompassed all his experiences, from his upbringing to his present struggles.

3. **Heavenly Judgment:**
Chris did not express fear of human judgment but focused instead on how his actions and life would be viewed in a spiritual or divine context. His concern was not about how society would judge him but how he would be judged in a heavenly court. This is reflected in his concern about whether he had been a good person in God's eyes, emphasizing the importance of spiritual integrity over societal approval.

4. **Accept Divine Sacrifice:**
Throughout his ordeal, Chris leaned heavily on his faith, particularly the concept of divine sacrifice. He accepted that Christ's sacrifice was central to his spiritual journey. This acceptance gave him strength and comfort, knowing his salvation was secured through Christ's death. This spiritual assurance played

a crucial role in how he navigated his illness, offering him hope and a sense of peace despite the challenges he faced.

5. **Acknowledge and Reject Wrongdoings:**

Chris's self-reflection included a deep acknowledgment of his past actions, particularly how he had treated others. He went as far as reaching out to people from his past to apologize for any wrongs he had committed. This step demonstrates his willingness to reject the undesired version of himself—prideful, independent to a fault—and embrace a more humble, open, and spiritually aware version of himself.

6. **Reconciliation in Christ:**

Chris found reconciliation in his relationship with Christ. His spiritual journey throughout his illness led him to a deeper reconciliation with God, as he accepted that he was spiritually renewed and forgiven. This reconciliation was not just about being absolved of past wrongdoings but also about embracing a new way of living that focused on helping others and living in alignment with his faith.

7. **Certainty of Eternal Life:**

Perhaps the most significant theme in Chris's story is the certainty of eternal life. The realization that life is finite led Chris to focus on what truly matters—his relationships, faith, and legacy. He accepted the certainty of death but found peace in the belief that there is life beyond this one. This certainty allowed him to approach his terminal illness w ith a sense of calm and purpose, using his remaining time to help others through the Guardian Knight Cancer Foundation.

Major Takeaways for Other Cancer Survivors
1. **Community and Support:** Accept help from others and value relationships for emotional strength.
2. **Spiritual Reflection and Growth:** Deepen your faith and reevaluate life priorities to find true fulfillment.
3. **Mental and Emotional Resilience:** Focus on the present, acknowledge emotional struggles, and seek support.
4. **Purpose and Legacy:** Find purpose in adversity and consider the legacy you want to leave.
5. **Financial Realities of Cancer:** Prepare financially and advocate for better access to care.
6. **Hope and Resilience:** Embrace the clarity of mortality to live fully and find strength in faith.
7. **The Power of Gratitude:** Appreciate small things and embrace gratitude for life to improve well-being.

CLEARING THE CLUTTER

REFLECTIONS

A JOURNEY OF FAITH AND AWARENESS:
OVERCOMING PROSTATE CANCER

By Dr. Carvason Griffith

While the doctors and treatments were essential, my ultimate healing would come from God.

I was born in the rural village of Josey Hill, St. Lucy Parish, in Barbados. People in town would often joke that we lived "behind God's back," far removed from the more developed areas. But for me, being "behind God's back" was a place of immense blessings. Though we were poor and isolated, my upbringing was filled with faith, hard work, and dreams of something greater.

My parents had very little formal education—my mother finished sixth grade, and my father even less. Yet, they set high expectations for us. My mother, the first in our village to join the Seventh-day Adventist Church, instilled a sense of faith and purpose in us. She often quoted scripture, telling us that

God's people should be the head and not the tail. That faith and determination fueled me to push beyond our circumstances.

After completing secondary school in Barbados, I worked in various jobs, including teaching and as a lab technician. Despite not receiving the scholarship I had hoped for, I never gave up on my dream of becoming a doctor. I eventually found my way to Oakwood College in Alabama, where I nurtured my faith while preparing for medical school. Oakwood was a sanctuary for me, a place where I could focus on both academic excellence and my spiritual growth. I flourished because I was surrounded by mentors and peers who shared my belief in God.

My choice to specialize in obstetrics and gynecology was inspired by my mother, who had delivered babies in our village. Her midwifery work and my experience in hospital labs analyzing pap smears gave me a passion for women's health. Over my 37-year career in Oklahoma City, I delivered roughly 9,000 babies. Each birth reaffirmed my faith in the miracle of life. But there were also challenges—moments of crisis when complications arose, and I found myself praying for guidance in the operating room. God always provided, carrying me through those difficult moments.

After retiring, I moved to Texas to be near my daughter, and it was there that I faced one of my toughest personal battles—prostate cancer. Having a medical background, I was proactive about my health, especially since my older brother had already been diagnosed with prostate cancer. I kept a close watch on my PSA levels, a key marker for prostate issues. While the doctors considered my levels to be within a normal range, I noticed a slow, steady increase over time. I knew something wasn't right, even before the official diagnosis.

Getting the diagnosis confirmed what I had suspected for a while. It was a strange moment—though I wasn't shocked, it still felt surreal to hear the word "cancer" associated with my health. But I had been preparing myself for this possibility, both mentally and spiritually. My wife, Frederica, was by my side from the very beginning. We prayed together, asking for God's guidance, and her unwavering faith strengthened mine. Having a praying, supportive wife was one of the greatest blessings throughout this journey. She helped me hold on to hope when fear tried to creep in, and together, we placed the situation in God's hands.

My experience as a doctor helped me navigate the medical side of things, but I knew that cancer was not just a physical battle—it was a test of faith. I had options for treatment, but each came with its risks and challenges. The doctors presented surgery and radiation as the primary options, but through my research, I discovered proton beam therapy, a more targeted and less invasive form of radiation. I was particularly drawn to this treatment because it offered fewer side effects, especially concerning issues like bowel problems, which are common with traditional radiation.

I found a proton beam therapy center in Irving, Texas, and after thoroughly investigating the doctors' credentials and experience with this form of treatment, I felt at peace with my decision. The treatment lasted about nine weeks, five days a week, with 44 sessions. Although it was demanding, it didn't incapacitate me. I maintained my daily routine, albeit with some fatigue and side effects.

One of the most challenging aspects was the hormone therapy that preceded the radiation. To reduce the cancer's fuel—testosterone—I was given injections that temporarily suppressed my hormone levels. This triggered severe hot flashes, something I had only heard about from my female patients going through menopause. Now, I could fully empathize with them. It was uncomfortable, but it gave me new insight into what others endure.

Throughout the treatment, my family stood by me. My wife's prayers and our shared faith in God kept me grounded, and the support of my entire family gave me the strength to face each day. I remained focused on God, believing that, while the doctors and treatments were essential, my ultimate healing would come from God. Every day, Frederica and I prayed for guidance and thanked Him for the medical advancements available to me. I never felt alone in this journey—God was with us every step of the way.

One day, I received a call from my sister, who reminded me of a truth that stayed with me throughout the process: it wasn't the treatment that would heal me, but God. Her words echoed in my mind as I navigated through the medical decisions. Soon after, a Urologist friend of my son reached out to offer advice and encouragement. He, too, reinforced my belief that I should trust God above all. These moments of affirmation strengthened my faith and reassured me that I was on the right path.

The treatment concluded, and the results were positive. I thanked God for guiding me through the process, for my wife's prayers, and for the strength to endure the challenges that came with it. The experience deepened my faith, reminding me that even in our darkest moments, God is present, leading us toward healing and restoration.

For those facing prostate cancer, my advice is this: never lose faith. Trust in God's plan, educate yourself about your health and don't be afraid to advocate for the care you need. As men, we often neglect our health, thinking we are invincible. But early detection, regular check-ups, and staying informed can save lives. Know your family history, and most importantly, lean on God for strength.

As I reflect on my journey—from a small village in Barbados to a career in medicine to surviving cancer—I can see the hand of God in every aspect of my life. His blessings were never behind His back but always present, guiding me toward His purpose. And for that, I am eternally grateful.

SPIRITUAL DECLUTTERING:

1. **Recognize Divine Record-Keeping**

Dr. Griffith's faith in God's omniscience is evident throughout his story. He acknowledges that God has kept a perfect record of his life, including his medical achievements, family life, and even his battles with cancer. He recognizes that God sees the full picture of his struggles and triumphs, both spiritually and professionally.

2. **Embrace God's Perspective**

Dr. Griffith embraces that God's perspective is broader than human understanding. He reflects on his upbringing, his career in medicine, and his battle with cancer, knowing that God understands the societal and familial context in which he grew up. From his humble beginnings in Barbados to his success as a doctor, he acknowledges that God has overseen his journey. This helps him put his life events into perspective, trusting in God's plan for him, even in times of illness.

3. Heavenly Judgment

Dr. Griffith accepts that God's judgment is not based on human measures of success but on divine understanding. He finds comfort in knowing that his life, including triumphs, challenges, and uncertainties, is being assessed by God's just and merciful standards rather than human judgment. His career, his service to others, and his cancer diagnosis are part of a divine record meant for heavenly judgment.

4. Accept Divine Sacrifice

The belief in Christ's sacrifice is central to Dr. Griffith's spiritual life. His faith in God's plan for salvation is reflected in how he approaches his cancer treatment. He trusts that he has been granted grace and the possibility of eternal life through Christ's sacrifice. He relies on this belief to find peace amid his health struggles, knowing that his relationship with God is what will ultimately matter.

5. Acknowledge and Reject Wrongdoings

Though Dr. Griffith has lived a life of service, especially as a physician who has delivered thousands of babies, he is aware of his shortcomings. He acknowledges that his mistakes, like all human wrongdoings, contributed to Christ's sacrifice. By rejecting his imperfections and striving for spiritual growth, he reinforces his commitment to living according to God's will.

6. **Reconciliation in Christ**

Dr. Griffith accepts that he is reconciled in Christ. He embraces God's forgiveness, which strengthens him during his battle with cancer. This reconciliation gives him peace, knowing that despite any failings or struggles in life, he has been made whole through Christ's grace. His decision-making process, including his treatment options, is rooted in this reconciliation, where he trusts that God's plan for his life is already established.

7. **Certainty of Eternal Life**

One of the most profound aspects of Dr. Griffith's cancer journey is his certainty in eternal life. He approaches his illness with the understanding that, no matter the outcome, his faith guarantees him a place with God. This certainty helps him face the challenges of cancer, knowing that even if his physical body is affected, his spiritual life is secure. He sees his treatment as part of God's will and trusts in a positive outcome, whether in this life or the next.

Major Takeaways for Other Cancer Survivors

1. **Faith as a Foundation:** Dr. Griffith's faith in God gave him peace and strength during his cancer journey, showing how spiritual or personal faith can be a vital source of hope for survivors.
2. **Proactive Self-Advocacy:** His medical knowledge and intuition led to early cancer detection. This highlights the importance of knowing your body, trusting your instincts, and advocating for your health.

3. **Informed Decision-Making:** Dr. Griffith researched and considered all treatment options, emphasizing the need for survivors to be well-informed and make choices aligned with their values and goals.
4. **Support from Family and Community:** A strong support system of family, friends, and colleagues provided emotional and practical help, making the journey less isolating.
5. **Spiritual Reflection and Clarity:** His diagnosis prompted deep spiritual reflection, helping him focus on what truly mattered in life, a process that can benefit other survivors.
6. **Embracing Uncertainty with Trust:** Dr. Griffith accepted the uncertainties of his journey with trust in God, suggesting that faith or personal beliefs can bring calm and strength in difficult times.

REFLECTIONS

A PATH OF PURPOSE:
FROM ZAMBIA TO BATTLING CANCER

By David Nkoma

I wasn't interested in vague prayers for good health.
I wanted specific, targeted prayers for healing.

My name is David Nkoma, and my life has been a testament to resilience, faith, and gratitude. I was born and raised in Zambia, where tradition runs deep and where I first learned the art of problem-solving. Whether fixing a broken tractor or mending a leaking water pipe, I discovered satisfaction in solving problems that made things work again. Little did I know that these early lessons in perseverance would be a lifeline in the battles ahead.

As I grew, I became fascinated with the idea of fixing not just machines but people. That curiosity led me to nursing, a career path that defied the expectations of my culture, where men were assumed to be doctors and women nurses. I stepped into this world more out of curiosity than anything else, unaware of what it would demand of me. But as I cared for newborns taking their first breaths and comforted those taking their last, I found a deep passion for the work. My journey took me through different fields—maternal and child health, oncology, cardiac care, and eventually, dialysis and infusion therapy. I spent over four decades caring for others, believing this was my calling and purpose.

In Zambia, healthcare was simple but constrained by a lack of resources. We did what we could with what we had. I remember a patient needing medicine made from a specific tree bark. We couldn't just take it all at once, or the tree would die. We had to respect the balance of nature, harvesting only what we needed, believing that even nature required care and understanding. Explaining this to people wasn't always easy, as old taboos often clashed with science. But we found a way to heal with what we had, guided by both tradition and necessity.

When I moved to the United States, I was struck by the stark differences in healthcare. Here, everything you could possibly need was available, but access came with a heavy price. In Zambia, we struggled to treat people because we lacked supplies. In America, I saw people being denied care because they lacked the money to pay for it. I watched as patients were asked for their insurance cards before being asked about their symptoms, and it pained me to see that this system, too, had its own kind of limitations.

For many years, I had been the caregiver. Then, in a cruel twist of fate, the roles were reversed. At nearly 61 years old, I was diagnosed with non-Hodgkin's lymphoma of the stomach. It all began with what I thought was a routine screening for colon cancer. I mentioned some stomach issues to my doctor, and he quickly ordered an endoscopy. I'll never forget the look on his face when I woke up from the procedure. His eyes were filled with worry as he said, "I don't like what I saw in your stomach." My heart sank. At that moment, my world shifted on its axis. I was no longer the healer; I was the one who needed healing.

I had always considered myself strong—physically, mentally, spiritually. But this diagnosis hit me like a sledgehammer. My four older brothers had all passed away before they turned 55, and here I was, nearly 61, facing a future that seemed uncertain. I felt like I had overstayed my welcome on this earth, as if I was living in "extra time," like in a football match, beyond what I had thought was my allotted time. The thought of leaving my family, not being there for my sons, young daughter, and my wife, Judith, was unbearable.

In those dark moments, I turned to my faith. I didn't hide my diagnosis; instead, I reached out to my church family and friends, asking them for their prayers. I wasn't interested in vague prayers for good health. I wanted specific, targeted prayers for healing, for a second chance at life. With all my heart, I believed that I could be healed with God's help.

The prayers began that very weekend, and by Monday, something remarkable had happened. My dangerously low hemoglobin levels rose from 11 to 12.5 without any medication. Some might call this a coincidence, but I knew it was more than that. It was a sign that the prayers were working, a glimmer of hope in the darkness.

The road to recovery was anything but smooth. Chemotherapy took a brutal toll on my body. In less than six months, I watched myself shrink from a healthy 210 pounds to a frail 115 pounds. My fingers went numb, and my feet felt like they were on fire every moment of the day. But through the pain and the weakness, I chose to see these sensations as reminders that I was still alive. Cancer had not won. I was still here, still fighting.

Navigating the healthcare system was another battle entirely. My oncologist recommended a staging CAT scan, but my insurance company refused to authorize it because I hadn't had a chest X-ray in the past six months. It didn't matter that I didn't need one; bureaucracy demanded it. I ended up paying for the scan out of pocket, draining my finances. But what choice did I have? I needed treatment, and time wasn't on my side.

The financial strain was overwhelming. After years of working to provide for my family, I faced bills I couldn't afford. My sons and Judith stood by me, but I could see the worry in their eyes. They tried to be strong, but I knew this was as hard for them as it was for me. Watching me, the man who had always been their rock, now frail and vulnerable, was breaking their hearts.

When chemotherapy finally ended, the doctors declared me in remission. But I didn't see it as just remission; I saw it as healing, a gift from God, an answer to the prayers lifted up on my behalf. Though I have lasting side effects—numbness in my fingers, burning in my feet—I consider them small prices to pay for the miracle of my life.

Life after cancer is different. I no longer take anything for granted. Every moment with my family, every conversation, every walk outside is precious. I've learned to live fully, appreciate the small details, and cherish my time with the people I love. Today, I am symptom-free. Some may call it luck or medical success, but I call it faith. I continue to walk this path, mindful of the lessons I've learned. My story isn't just about surviving cancer; it's about living with purpose, embracing each day as a gift, and never losing hope.

DECLUTTERING

1. **Recognize Divine Record-Keeping**

David's faith journey begins with his acceptance that God, not humans, holds the ultimate record of his life. His life in Zambia, his journey into healthcare, his work helping others, and his struggles are all recognized as part of God's divine plan. He expresses deep humility in acknowledging that his life's events, including both the good and bad, are known to God. This realization leads him to a clear evaluation of his spiritual condition as he faces his diagnosis, knowing that a higher power is recording his story.

2. **Embrace God's Perspective**

Throughout his narrative, David accepts God's universal understanding of human nature and societal context. His upbringing in Zambia, with its strong cultural beliefs, contrasts sharply with his experiences in the U.S. healthcare system, yet he understands these experiences as part of a broader plan. He accepts his journey from a farm boy fixing machinery to a healthcare provider and, later, a patient. By embracing this divine perspective, David demonstrates how he has come to see his life as part of a larger spiritual framework shaped by God's understanding of the world he was born into.

3. Heavenly Judgment

David's illness forces him to reflect on the fragility of life. He acknowledges that his life and actions will be judged not by human standards but in a heavenly court. When faced with a terminal illness, he understands that God, not earthly institutions, will weigh his past actions, his service as a nurse, and his personal faith. This sense of heavenly judgment brings him peace, as he knows that his life story will be interpreted in the divine context.

4. Accept Divine Sacrifice

David's belief in the Christian concept of salvation becomes the foundation of his coping mechanism. In the face of cancer, he reaches out to his Christian community, asking for prayers and placing his hope in God's grace and the sacrifice of Jesus Christ. He prays for a second chance, mirroring his acceptance of Christ's substitutionary death and the rewards promised to those who accept Him. David understands that his survival is not in his hands but in God's, and he submits to God's will.

5. Acknowledge and Reject Wrongdoings

Though the narrative does not delve deeply into specific wrongdoings, David's story suggests a self-awareness of his imperfections. His humility in seeking prayer and help from others indicates his acceptance of his human limitations and the acknowledgment that his life has been imperfect. However, instead of dwelling on these wrongs, he rejects this flawed version of himself, placing his faith in God's ability to heal and transform him.

6. Reconciliation in Christ

David believes that his life and illness are reconciled in Christ. Despite the physical toll of chemotherapy and the uncertainty surrounding his health, David finds strength in his belief that he has been reconciled through faith. He recognizes that cancer, though debilitating, is not the end of his story. His faith assures him that whatever happens, his life has been made whole through Christ, which gives him the courage to continue living with purpose.

7. Certainty of Eternal Life

The certainty of eternal life is a central theme in David's story. He views his battle with cancer through the lens of faith, believing that even if cancer had taken his life, he would still have hope in eternal life. David compares his life to a football match, where he believes he has entered "extra time." He knows that life is fragile, and his faith in eternal life allows him to see his illness not as an end but as part of a divine plan. His confidence in God's promise of eternal life helps him approach each day with a positive mindset, seeing his recovery not just as physical healing but as spiritual renewal.

Major Takeaways for Other Cancer Survivors

1. **Faith and Spiritual Strength:** Spiritual grounding, whether through religious faith or personal beliefs, can provide comfort and resilience during treatment.
2. **The Importance of Community Support:** Surround yourself with a supportive network of family, friends, and community members who can offer encouragement and practical help.
3. **Open Communication:** Be open and honest about your diagnosis and needs, which can enhance the support you receive from others.
4. **Mental Resilience:** Maintain a positive mindset and focus on small victories to help sustain hope during tough times.
5. **The Role of Perseverance:** Endure and push through obstacles, whether they are physical, emotional, or bureaucratic, to ensure your survival and recovery.
6. **Accepting Help from Others:** Don't hesitate to accept emotional, spiritual, or practical support from others; it's a crucial part of healing.
7. **Self-Acceptance and Living with Side Effects:** Accept that life post-treatment may come with lasting changes, but these do not diminish the value of life.
8. **Focus on the Present:** Value and appreciate the present moment, which can help ground you and reduce anxiety about the future.
9. **Persistence in Healthcare Advocacy:** Be your own advocate within the healthcare system to ensure you receive the necessary care.

FROM ZAMBIA TO BATTLING CANCER

REFLECTIONS

FROM JAMAICA TO NIH:
MY UNYIELDING JOURNEY

By Kinte Mendes

I reminded myself that I was fighting for something bigger than just my own survival.

I never imagined that cancer would become a part of my life's story. Yet, here I am, a living testament to the unpredictable paths life can take us on. My journey has been one of soaring highs and devastating lows, marked by an unyielding resilience, a stubborn hope, and a determination that refuses to be extinguished. I've faced many battles before, but none quite like this. Born with a few health complications, I thought I'd seen the worst after surviving a harrowing car accident in Jamaica in 1999 and undergoing a difficult cataract surgery in 2006. I enjoyed relatively good health for years, thinking I had left the worst behind me. But life had other plans.

It was around 2011 that things began to change. I noticed a strange darkening around my eyes and ears. Thinking it was just an allergy, my doctor suggested I adjust my diet. I did, but nothing seemed to help. The darkness spread, and by 2014, those spots had turned into unsightly bumps that seemed to grow out of nowhere. Desperate for answers, I turned to a dermatologist friend who removed them but didn't see the need for a biopsy. Little did we know, this was only the beginning of a nightmare that would turn my world upside down.

By 2017, the swelling was worse, and by 2018, it was undeniable that something was seriously wrong. What we once considered simple allergies had now transformed into a grim reality. A biopsy revealed lymphoid hyperplasia, and soon after, my vision started to blur. I went from specialist to specialist, hoping for answers, for a miracle. But none came. Instead, I was met with confusion, uncertainty, and fear. And then, the news that shattered everything: a second biopsy confirmed that I had acute T-cell lymphoma, a rare and aggressive form of cancer. Cancer. Me? I could hardly process it. It felt like my world was collapsing around me, but I knew I had to face this battle head-on, no matter how terrified I was.

I began my treatment journey at Kingston University Hospital of the West Indies (UHWI). CHOP chemotherapy was the recommended course, and though I tried to brace myself for the journey ahead, nothing could have prepared me for what was to come. After just two doses, my body rebelled. I developed a painful abscess, and the treatment had to be halted. Each time the lymphoma returned, it seemed more determined, more aggressive, like a dark shadow that wouldn't let go. The doctors decided we needed a more aggressive approach. It felt like a race against time, and I was running out of it.

Navigating the Jamaican healthcare system was a battle in itself. Tests and treatments were prohibitively expensive, and my insurance company initially refused to cover my treatment. I felt helpless, suffocated by the weight of it all. But in my darkest hour, my high school classmates from Munro College, friends, and community rallied around me. Together, we raised enough funds for my medication, though I still had to travel across Jamaica to find the right pharmacies. The outpouring of support was overwhelming, a lifeline that kept me afloat when I felt like I was drowning.

Then, like a beacon of hope in the storm, I received a call from Dr. Nicole Urquhart, a coordinator at the National Institutes of Health (NIH) in the United States. She offered me the chance to participate in a clinical trial, a lifeline I desperately needed. At first, I was hesitant. The idea of clinical trials felt daunting as if I were a guinea pig. But I realized this was more than just a chance to save my own life—it was an opportunity to contribute to medical research that could help others. I decided to take that leap of faith.

In December 2018, I flew to the United States for the first time, carrying with me all the hopes and prayers of my loved ones. The experience at NIH was unlike anything I had ever known. I was thrown into a whirlwind of tests, scans, and treatments—from radiation therapy to immunotherapy. The side effects were brutal: fevers that left me shivering, hives that covered my body, and itching so unbearable I wanted to claw my skin off. But through it all, I reminded myself that I was fighting for something bigger than just my own survival. I was fighting for others who might benefit from the knowledge gained through my journey, fighting for those who would come after me.

By March 2019, I was sent back home to Jamaica. The doctors were hopeful; my pulmonary embolism, which had developed during treatment, had miraculously disappeared. For the first time in what felt like forever, I could see a sliver of light at the end of this dark tunnel. Things seemed to be looking up. I even returned to work in September of that year, slowly trying to piece together the life that cancer had tried to take from me.

But cancer is a relentless enemy. In December 2019, just as I began to feel like myself again, I noticed a familiar swelling in my ears. My heart sank. It was back. The disease that had tried to claim me once before was making its return. And then, as if the universe wasn't done testing me, the pandemic hit. My path back to the NIH for further treatment was blocked, and I was left stranded in Jamaica, knowing that the cancer was growing and spreading while I waited helplessly for flights to resume.

I finally returned to the NIH in July 2020 only to face another challenge. My cataracts, worsened by the treatments, had left me almost completely blind. I felt like I was losing everything—my sight, my health, my hope. But I underwent surgery to restore my vision and, once recovered, resumed my battle against cancer with a determination fiercer than ever before. The road was long and filled with pain, but by October 2020, I was sent home once again.

Through it all, I've learned so much about resilience, the power of a strong support system, and the vital role of medical research. My story is one of survival against all odds. I know I still live with the possibility of relapse, but I wake up each day grateful for the time I have been given. I hope my journey can inspire others to keep fighting, no matter how impossible the battle may seem. Because even in the darkest of times, there is always a flicker of hope, a reason to keep moving forward, a life worth living.

DECLUTTERING

1. **Recognize Divine Record-Keeping:**

Kinte frequently contemplates his situation in a deeply reflective manner. Although he does not directly reference divine record-keeping, his prayers and reflections about his life's impact implicitly acknowledge that his actions, thoughts, and efforts are observed beyond the human realm. His questions about what he has done for mankind indicate an awareness that his life story is being evaluated not just by others but by a higher power. Kinte is aware of a higher purpose and reflects on how his life has been meaningful beyond his personal experience.

2. **Embrace God's Perspective:**

Kinte's journey reveals an evolving understanding of his human limitations and the broader context of his suffering. When he acknowledges the possibility of his death and says, "What if what I do can benefit mankind?" he accepts a larger, divine perspective. This outlook reveals a surrender to God's broader plan for his life, seeing beyond the immediate physical suffering and focusing on how his experience could benefit others. Kinte embraces the notion that his suffering has a greater purpose and that his life is part of a larger divine plan.

3. **Heavenly Judgment:**

Kinte's mindset reveals that he is not overly concerned with human judgments or societal expectations but focuses more on what matters in the spiritual realm. He shows little concern for worldly status or success, concentrating instead on the personal meaning of his suffering and the possibility of contributing to humanity's collective understanding of the disease. His acceptance of his condition without seeking human approval highlights this theme of divine judgment. Kinte focuses on living according to a spiritual purpose rather than seeking worldly validation.

4. **Accept Divine Sacrifice:**

In moments of deep prayer, Kinte understands that he is living in God's grace and hopes for a place in heaven ("Lord, you said in your Father's house there are many mansions. I hope you would prepare one for me"). He accepts God's sacrifice and expresses faith in eternal reward, reflecting his acceptance of God's substitutionary role in his salvation and ultimate outcome. Kinte accepts his mortality and places his hope in divine sacrifice, finding solace in the promise of eternal life.

5. **Acknowledge and Reject Wrongdoings:**

While Kinte doesn't directly dwell on his wrongdoings, his reflections on his life seem to involve a sense of responsibility and self-examination. His desire to do something beneficial for mankind could be interpreted as acknowledging past shortcomings or missed opportunities. His desire to contribute positively throughout his last days reflects a form of rejecting a past version of himself that he perceives as unfulfilled. Kinte undergoes self-examination and seeks to redefine his legacy by contributing meaningfully to the world.

6. **Reconciliation in Christ:**

Kinte's faith is present throughout his journey, especially in his prayers. He expresses a sense of peace and reconciliation with his fate, showing that he has made peace with God. His acceptance of the uncertainty of his survival and his willingness to participate in a clinical trial, even if it might not benefit him personally, reflects a deep spiritual reconciliation. Kinte achieves a sense of spiritual peace and acceptance, reconciling his suffering and fate with his faith in Christ.

7. **Certainty of Eternal Life:**

Despite his fears and struggles, Kinte's journey reflects a profound belief in eternal life. His prayer for a place in heaven and his focus on doing something that benefits mankind show his hope for an existence beyond the physical realm. He is not fixated on survival but on making his life count spiritually and ensuring his soul is in alignment with God. Kinte finds hope and strength in the certainty of eternal life, using his suffering to grow spiritually and help others.

Major Takeaways for Other Cancer Survivors

1. **Persistence in Seeking the Right Diagnosis and Treatment:** Advocate for your health by seeking multiple opinions and not settling for inadequate explanations. Early and accurate diagnosis is crucial.

2. **Navigating Healthcare Systems with Support:** Build and lean on a support system of family, friends, and community to help navigate healthcare challenges and access necessary treatments.
3. **Exploring Clinical Trials:** Be open to clinical trials and new treatment options, as they can provide cutting-edge treatments and contribute to medical research.
4. **Facing Adversity with Faith:** Draw strength from faith or personal beliefs to navigate the emotional and spiritual challenges of a cancer diagnosis.
5. **Maintaining Hope While Preparing for Uncertainty:** Balance hope with acceptance of uncertainty to find emotional peace and make your journey meaningful.
6. **Importance of Resilience and Adaptability:** Cultivate resilience by adapting to physical, emotional, and logistical challenges, focusing on overcoming them step by step.
7. **The Power of Positive Impact:** View your battle as part of a larger story, contributing to medical advancements and inspiring others by sharing your journey.
8. **Use of Natural Remedies with Medical Care:** Consider integrating natural remedies with medical treatments, but always consult with healthcare professionals.

MY UNYIELDING JOURNEY

REFLECTIONS

A NEW BEGINNING:
MY STORY OF STRENGTH AND RECOVERY

By Kinte Mendes

It was a long, grueling process, but every step I took was a victory, no matter how small.

I vividly remember that day, like it was etched into my memory with fire. It was October 29th, the day before my birthday, and instead of celebrating, I found myself back in Jamaica after another round of intravenous treatments. My birthday passed in a blur of exhaustion, spent in bed, a stark reminder of the relentless fight ahead. By December 2020, I was back at work, trying to find some semblance of normalcy. But things weren't the same. My body was weak, and even though I followed all the protocols for treatment and medical leave, I went unpaid for months. It felt like the world was closing in on me from every direction. The school board, which had once been supportive, had now turned their backs on me. I felt betrayed and alone, fighting not just for my health but for my livelihood as well.

I fought back with everything I had, including my union and the public defender. It felt like I was battling on every front—my body, mind, job. Just when it seemed like all hope was lost, they relented. I won that battle, but it was just one of many.

The doctors kept a close eye on me, monitoring my condition with every test and scan they could think of. But my body wasn't responding as they had hoped to the three rounds of treatment I'd undergone—CHOP, immunotherapy, and so much more. It was as if the cancer was mocking our efforts, growing stronger each time we tried to fight it back. That's when they brought up the idea of a stem cell transplant. It felt like a crossroads, a potential turning point in this grueling journey. But there was a problem: I needed a suitable donor.

I reached out to my family, hoping and praying that someone would be a match. My brother was the first to be tested, but wasn't a match. My parents were too old to be donors. Like sand, I felt hope slipping through my fingers as I contacted cousins and half-siblings. Each phone call and test brought back the same heartbreaking result: no match. It wasn't until my full sister, Amma, stepped up that we found an 80% match. She was in the U.S., and without hesitation, she traveled to the National Institutes of Health (NIH) to undergo all the necessary health checks. I'll never forget the relief that washed over me when I found out she was healthy enough to donate. They harvested her stem cells and froze them, waiting for the day when I could return for the transplant. It felt like we were on the brink of something miraculous, but the waiting was agonizing.

The days leading up to the transplant were some of the longest of my life. My blood pressure spiked, probably from the anxiety that gripped me like a vice. Every time the nurses came to check on me, I could see the concern in their eyes and feel the tension in the air. January 12th, 2022—D-Day, they called it. I was prepped and ready, though fear and hope battled for space in my heart. As they pumped my sister's stem cells into me, I couldn't help but think this could be my second birthday, a rebirth of sorts. For a brief moment, I felt fine, even hopeful. But it didn't take long before the side effects hit me like a freight train. Vomiting, chills, fever—I was caught in a storm that raged inside my body. I was so weak, so tired. There were days when I wondered if I would ever recover and if this would be my new normal.

I couldn't even walk. I had to relearn how to move, one painful step at a time. The nurses were like guardian angels, guiding and encouraging me as I stumbled and struggled to find my footing. At first, just a few steps left me gasping for breath, but I was determined. I couldn't let this disease take everything from me. Slowly, painfully, I regained some strength. I walked around the ward with their assistance and then started doing exercises on my own. It was a long, grueling process, but every step I took was a victory, no matter how small.

There were times when I felt utterly alone, but I wasn't. My friend Jennifer Hendricks, the social worker, was there for me in ways I never expected. She brought me meals, but more importantly, she helped coordinate my girlfriend's visa so she could come and be with me. Having her there was a comfort, a reminder that I wasn't just a patient but a person who was loved and cared for. Even though my appetite was nearly nonexistent and food tasted strange, having homemade Jamaican dishes brought a small sense of normalcy back into my life.

By June 2022, I was back in Jamaica. But the journey was far from over. In August, I started feeling weak and dizzy again. I knew something was wrong, so I went to the hospital, suspecting graft-versus-host disease. When I explained my situation, the doctor looked at me in shock—stem cell transplants were unheard of in Jamaica. They referred me to the University Hospital for further tests, but the delays were frustrating. It felt like I was racing against time, and every second was slipping away. Eventually, I returned to the NIH for treatment, but the uncertainty was suffocating.

And then, just when I thought I was in the clear, I was hit with another blow. I contracted COVID-19. The irony wasn't lost on me—the pandemic had officially ended, and here I was, having survived cancer and a stem cell transplant, now fighting a virus that had shaken the world. I braced myself for the worst, but by some miracle, I had no severe symptoms. Still, they isolated me, treating me as though I were radioactive, and once again, I felt the crushing weight of isolation.

By May 2023, I returned home, having survived both the transplant and COVID. In the months that followed, I underwent more tests, including bone marrow extractions, which showed no evidence of cancer. Today, I feel stronger and healthier than I have in years. It's been an incredible journey—one marked by pain, uncertainty, and moments of overwhelming gratitude. The doctors, nurses, and NIH staff saved my life, and for that, I am forever grateful.

Looking back, I see a story of survival—of fighting through the darkness and finding light on the other side. It's a story of love, community, and faith that held me up when I felt like falling down. Though the journey continues, I face each day with a heart full of hope and gratitude, knowing that every moment is a gift.

DECLUTTERING

1. **Recognize Divine Record-Keeping**

Kinte's battle with illness involved numerous moments where he faced mortality and uncertainty. His recounting of events shows a deep awareness of his life's narrative and an understanding that a higher power observed every trial and triumph. Whether he expressed it explicitly or implicitly, the sense of divine oversight seems present in how he reflects on his experiences, showing an acceptance that his suffering, perseverance, and resilience are all part of a larger, divinely observed record.

2. **Embrace God's Perspective**

Kinte's story, particularly the patience and faith he exhibited through various treatments and delays, shows a recognition that there is a broader, divine understanding of his journey. He seemed to accept that his trials were part of something bigger than himself, indicating a recognition that his story—though filled with hardship—was seen and understood by a higher power. His patience during medical and bureaucratic delays shows that he embraced a sense of divine timing rather than succumbing to frustration.

3. **Heavenly Judgment**

Kinte may not speak explicitly about judgment, but the undertones of his journey reflect an understanding that his life's trials were not for human judgment but part of a greater spiritual journey. His focus on survival, treatment, and faith reflects a belief that his story is ultimately measured on a divine scale, not just a human one. His calmness, even in moments of extreme physical vulnerability, shows an implicit acceptance of this larger spiritual evaluation.

4. Accept Divine Sacrifice

Although Kinte's story is focused on his medical battles, there is a spiritual undercurrent that suggests he accepts the idea of sacrifice and redemption. His struggle with cancer can be seen as a metaphor for accepting God's sacrifice, as he endures physical suffering but ultimately emerges stronger. His perseverance in seeking healing—even when hope seemed dim—aligns with the idea that spiritual endurance, aided by God's ultimate sacrifice, leads to a form of salvation.

5. Acknowledge and Reject Wrongdoings

Kinte does not dwell on wrongdoings, but his story reflects a rejection of despair and a commitment to moving forward, even when his body fails. He acknowledges the difficulties in his life, including the strain of battling his illness, but he rejects giving up or accepting defeat. This reflects the process of spiritual decluttering, where one acknowledges human failings but seeks a higher path of reconciliation and renewal.

6. Reconciliation in Christ

Kinte's story is marked by moments of deep uncertainty, yet it is clear that he finds reconciliation in his perseverance and faith. His gratitude for the medical professionals and his sister, who became his stem cell donor, indicates an awareness of grace and love present in his life. His eventual healing and recovery echo a reconciliation with life and with God, signifying a form of spiritual peace after an intense struggle.

7. **Certainty of Eternal Life**

By the end of his narrative, Kinte speaks of his healing and recovery with a sense of hope and resilience. He survived cancer, endured a stem cell transplant, and even overcame contracting COVID during his recovery. His strength and calmness in facing these challenges reflect a spiritual certainty that he has been given more time. This hope and optimism for the future and his acknowledgment of his blessings signify a belief in eternal life and divine favor after enduring so many hardships.

Major Takeaways for Other Cancer Survivors

1. **Faith and Resilience:** Maintain hope and spiritual resilience, even when facing extreme suffering.
2. **Community and Support:** Embrace support from family, friends, and healthcare teams; don't isolate yourself.
3. **Trusting the Process:** Be patient and trust both medical and spiritual processes, even when healing is slow.
4. **Gratitude in Small Victories:** Appreciate small acts of kindness and blessings to stay grounded.
5. **Overcoming Fear:** Face fears head-on, whether about mortality or treatment uncertainties and keep moving forward.

CLEARING THE CLUTTER

REFLECTIONS

FAITH AND FORTITUDE:
NAVIGATING LIFE'S UNEXPECTED TURNS

By Priscilla Jones

Faith, I've realized, isn't just about praying for healing. It's about trusting the process, even when it doesn't make sense.

I never thought I'd find myself here, sitting on my porch, reflecting on a journey I never asked for but have somehow learned to embrace with a sense of purpose. My name is Priscilla Jones, and in March of this year, my life took an unexpected, life-altering turn. I was diagnosed with triple-negative breast cancer—a diagnosis that felt like a punch to the gut, knocking the wind out of me and changing everything I thought I knew about my life.

I was just about to turn 40 and was already preparing for what I thought would be a significant life transition—becoming an empty nester as my youngest child headed off to college. I had imagined this time would be filled with new beginnings, a chance to rediscover myself after years of being a full-time mom. But life had other plans for me, plans I never saw coming.

It started on an ordinary, quiet evening. I was in bed, moments away from drifting off to sleep, when I rolled over and felt something strange in my breast. It was just a small lump, but something about it felt unsettling. At first, I tried to dismiss it, thinking it was probably nothing. But the thought nagged at me like an uninvited guest who refused to leave. I knew I couldn't ignore it, so I made an appointment with my new doctor, thinking it would be a routine check-up. After all, I hadn't even turned 40 yet, and cancer wasn't on my radar.

I went in for a mammogram, and then they told me I needed an ultrasound. I stayed positive, convinced it was probably just a cyst or something benign. But then they said I needed a biopsy, and that's when the reality started to sink in. I tried to hold on to hope. I had no symptoms—no pain, no discharge, nothing to suggest that something was seriously wrong. So, when the biopsy results came back confirming breast cancer, it felt like the ground was ripped out from under me.

I remember the call like it was yesterday. My doctor, bless his heart, called me outside of regular hours on a weekend to deliver the news. I could hear the urgency and compassion in his voice, and I knew it must be serious. Still, the words hit me like a ton of bricks. I felt numb, confused, and utterly lost. What was I supposed to do now? How could this be happening?

The days that followed were a whirlwind of doctor's appointments, treatment plans, and information overload. It was like being caught in a storm, trying to find my way without a map. I met with my oncologist, then my surgeon, and before I knew it, I was starting chemotherapy. Twelve rounds of chemo in my first cycle—each one a battle I never imagined I'd have to fight. The side effects were brutal, but I was determined. I tried to maintain my routine—eating healthy, staying active, and, most importantly, leaning on my faith.

Faith has always been a part of who I am. I've always been a calm, positive person, and while this journey has tested me in ways I never thought possible, it has also brought me closer to God. It's like walking through an unknown, frightening, and uncertain wilderness, but I've learned you can't run from it. You have to face it head-on, even when you feel like giving up. Faith, I've realized, isn't just about praying for healing. It's about trusting the process, even when it doesn't make sense. It's about believing that no matter what happens, you are exactly where you're meant to be and that there is a purpose in all of this, even if it's hidden in the pain.

My family has been my lifeline through all of this, especially my children. They've been my rock, reminding me daily to stay strong and keep pushing forward. My youngest, who is about to leave for college, has been a constant source of motivation. I tell her, "You go do your thing, and I'll be here fighting to make sure I'm there to see you graduate." That thought keeps me going on the hardest days when the weight of it all feels too much to bear.

Sharing my journey on TikTok was something I never expected to do, but it turned out to be one of my greatest blessings. When I was first diagnosed, I didn't know anyone personally who had gone through breast cancer, so I turned to social media, searching for support and understanding. I found a community of incredible women from all walks of life who have been where I am now. Their strength and courage gave me the courage to share my story. Now, I post regularly, hoping my journey can be a light for someone else going through the same thing. It's therapeutic for me, but more than that, it's a way to give back, to let others know they're not alone.

As I prepare to start my second cycle of chemotherapy, I'm filled with a mix of anxiety and hope. I've learned to advocate for myself, to speak up when something doesn't feel right, and to trust my body, even when it's struggling. Cancer may be a part of my story now, but it doesn't define me. It's just one chapter in a much larger book—a book filled with love, faith, and resilience.

This journey has taught me to appreciate the small things, to live in the moment, and to never take anything for granted. I've learned that I am stronger than I ever knew, that there is power in vulnerability, and that sometimes, the most difficult paths lead to the most beautiful destinations. So, as I sit here on my porch, watching the world go by, I am filled with gratitude: gratitude for my family, for my faith, and for the chance to keep fighting. Because as long as there's breath in my body, I will keep going. And that, I believe, is the greatest gift of all.

DECLUTTERING

1. Recognize Divine Record-Keeping

Priscilla recognizes that her life is under God's watchful care, even in moments of uncertainty, like her cancer diagnosis. She speaks of her faith and how it grounds her to trust that everything she is experiencing is part of a divine plan. This belief is central to her acceptance of the cancer journey as something beyond her control, allowing her to trust that God is aware of her struggles and victories, both internal and external.

2. **Embrace God's Perspective**

Priscilla embraces the idea that God understands the complexities of her life, including the societal and personal challenges she has faced, such as being a teenage mother and growing up with little parental support. She does not ask, "Why me?" but instead sees her journey, including her cancer, as part of a broader, divinely guided narrative. This acceptance reflects her belief that God's understanding of her human experience is far greater than hers.

3. **Heavenly Judgment**

Priscilla's focus is not on the judgment of others but on her relationship with God. She emphasizes that her cancer journey is helping her grow closer to God, reinforcing her belief that her life's meaning is ultimately determined by her Creator. This reflects a focus on heavenly rather than earthly judgments, where Priscilla finds peace knowing God knows her true self.

4. **Accept Divine Sacrifice**

While Priscilla doesn't explicitly delve into theological discussions about divine sacrifice, her faith-based journey suggests a deep connection to God's grace and mercy. She expresses gratitude for life and trusts in God's plan, which may reflect an implicit understanding of Christ's sacrifice and the hope it brings. Her belief that she is already healed, as she states, aligns with the idea of accepting divine sacrifice and redemption.

5. Acknowledge and Reject Wrongdoings

Priscilla doesn't dwell on past mistakes or wrongdoings in the interview but focuses on the lessons learned throughout her life. She speaks of how her upbringing and challenges have shaped her into a resilient and positive person. Her narrative suggests that she has accepted and moved beyond past hardships, focusing instead on the person she has become and her journey toward a better self through faith.

6. Reconciliation in Christ

Priscilla frequently references her faith as a source of peace and reconciliation. She sees her journey with cancer as part of God's plan to teach her something deeper about herself and her relationship with Him. This reflects the idea of being reconciled in Christ, as she accepts her situation gracefully and believes that her faith has brought her closer to God.

7. Certainty of Eternal Life

Priscilla exudes a strong belief in eternal life and the hope that transcends her current challenges. She explicitly states that she believes she is already healed, which aligns with the certainty of eternal life. This perspective allows her to face the challenges of her cancer diagnosis with a sense of peace and purpose, knowing that her life has meaning beyond her physical existence.

Major Takeaways for Other Cancer Survivors

1. **Faith as a Source of Strength:** Maintaining one's faith is instrumental in overcoming illness. Trusting in God's plan can provide strength and peace during uncertain times.

2. **Advocacy and Self-Awareness:** Understanding your body and being vocal about your needs is crucial. Trust your intuition and speak up when necessary.
3. **Positive Outlook and Resilience:** Choosing positivity can significantly impact healing and mental health, inspiring others to focus on hope and resilience.
4. **Acceptance of Life's Uncertainties:** Acceptance of one's diagnosis and focusing on the present highlight the importance of letting go of things beyond one's control. Embrace life's uncertainties with grace.
5. **Spiritual Growth and Reflection:** Aspiring for a deeper connection with God during one's journey can turn crises into opportunities for spiritual growth and reflection, helping survivors find deeper meaning and purpose.

CLEARING THE CLUTTER

REFLECTIONS

RESILIENT IN THE STORM:
A JOURNEY OF FAITH, STRENGTH, AND HOPE

By Khrysitin Mutton

Feel your emotions. Cry, grieve, scream if you need to, but don't stay there.

I had just turned 35, and life felt like it was finally coming together. That year, I had set a goal to be in the best shape of my life and was achieving it. My career flourished, my clientele grew, and everything seemed to align perfectly. But then, out of nowhere, life threw me a curveball.

It started subtly—a little fatigue, unexplained weight loss—but I dismissed the signs. "Maybe it's my anemia," I told myself. I was losing pounds overnight, far beyond what seemed normal. It was only after catching COVID-19 and struggling with shortness of breath that I went to the ER, thinking they'd prescribe antibiotics and send me home. Instead, the scans revealed a mass on my lung—almost the size of the lung itself. The words "Hodgkin's lymphoma" entered my life, and I felt like the ground had been ripped from beneath me.

At first, I was in denial. I joked to cope because that's what I do. But the truth hit me like a ton of bricks when I realized this wasn't just a bad dream. I confided in my family, each conversation filled with heartbreak and tears. My mom, ever the strong one, held her emotions back to support me. But I could see the pain in her eyes. My clients—who felt more like family—were there for me every step of the way. I was surrounded by love, but I often felt like I had to comfort them when I was the one battling cancer.

Chemotherapy began, and to my surprise, I tolerated it better than I had feared. I didn't experience the debilitating nausea many described. Instead, I faced unexpected side effects like discolored nails. I was tired but determined to maintain normalcy, so I continued working. It gave me purpose and reminded me of who I was beyond the diagnosis.

After six months, I completed treatment. We celebrated that day—I went out with my family, joyfully believing I was done with cancer. But within a week, my world crumbled again. The cancer was back. I spiraled into a deep, emotional place, questioning everything, even God. Everyone had told me how treatable Hodgkin's lymphoma was. Why, then, was it still here?

The second round of chemo was relentless, harsher, and crueler. I lost my hair, eyelashes, and eyebrows for the second time. Looking in the mirror, I didn't recognize myself. As a hairdresser, I knew how much hair represented femininity and identity. Losing it felt like losing a part of me. To cope, I wore wigs and makeup when I went out, trying to cling to some semblance of normalcy.

This journey has changed me in ways I never imagined. It stripped me of my illusions about life and what matters. The little things that consumed me—other people's opinions, trivial worries—have disappeared. Facing the fragility of life brought me closer to my family and God. I've learned that the strength I didn't think I had runs deep within me.

Today, I advocate for others. God has called me to share my story to comfort others in their battles. Through TikTok and other platforms, I've connected with a community of fighters who understand the pain, resilience, and hope that come with this journey. My advice to anyone facing cancer—or any challenge—is this: Feel your emotions. Cry, grieve, scream if you need to, but don't stay there. Keep going. Find the beauty in your reflection, even when it's hard to see. You are more than your outward appearance. You are strong, you are worthy, and you are loved.

This is not just a story of survival but of transformation. Cancer tried to break me, but it only made me stronger. My faith has deepened, my relationships have grown, and my purpose has become clear. This is my testimony.

DECLUTTERING

1. **Recognize Divine Record-Keeping**

    Khrystin's journey reflects an understanding that her story—every triumph, struggle, and tear—is recorded not by humans but by God. Even in her darkest moments, she expressed a deep sense of faith, recognizing that her pain had a purpose beyond her understanding. As she shared her testimony on platforms like TikTok, Khrystin acknowledged that her story was being used to inspire others, aligning her narrative with God's greater record-keeping.

2. **Embrace God's Perspective**

Khrystin wrestled with feelings of frustration and doubt, questioning why a second recurrence of cancer was part of her journey. Yet, she came to see her trials through God's broader perspective. She noted that her suffering brought her closer to her family, strengthened her faith, and allowed her to discover a resilience she hadn't known existed.

3. **Heavenly Judgment**

Khrystin's reflections on life reveal a deep awareness that her ultimate judgment comes from God, not society. Losing her hair—a symbol of her femininity and identity—forced her to confront and redefine her sense of self-worth. Through this process, she realized that her value was not determined by her physical appearance but by her spirit and faith.

4. **Accept Divine Sacrifice**

Throughout her journey, Khrystin leaned on her faith in Christ's sacrifice. She acknowledged moments of questioning God but ultimately found solace in His love and purpose for her life. This acceptance became a source of strength, allowing her to persevere through grueling treatments and emotional lows.

5. **Acknowledge and Reject Wrongdoings**

Khrystin's journey also involved self-reflection. She mentioned changing the way she spoke to herself, rejecting negativity, and learning to uplift herself through affirmations. This transformation reflected her rejection of self-doubt and fear, choosing instead to embrace God's truth about her worth and potential.

6. **Reconciliation in Christ**

Khrystin found reconciliation through her faith, recognizing that her battle was not only physical but also spiritual. She expressed gratitude for the closeness to God and family that her illness brought, seeing these as blessings that reconciled her to what truly matters.

7. **Certainty of Eternal Life**

Finally, Khrystin accepted the certainty of eternal life, finding peace in the knowledge that her suffering was temporary and her ultimate reward lay with God. This understanding allowed her to view her challenges as opportunities for growth rather than obstacles.

Major Takeaways for Other Cancer Survivors:

1. **It's Okay to Feel Broken—But Don't Stay There.** Embrace your emotions and allow yourself to grieve but remember to rise and keep moving forward. Healing comes when you choose not to remain in despair.
2. **Your Identity is More Than Your Appearance:** Cancer may change your appearance but doesn't diminish your value. True beauty and worth come from within.

3. **Surround Yourself with Supportive People:** Lean on your support system. Allow loved ones to be there for you, as their strength can help sustain you when yours feels depleted.
4. **Faith as a Source of Strength:** Faith can be a powerful anchor in times of uncertainty. Trusting in a higher purpose can transform fear and doubt into hope and resilience.
5. **Advocate for Yourself:** Be your own advocate in the healthcare system. Trust your instincts, ask questions, and ensure your voice is heard throughout your treatment journey.
6. **Positivity and Realism Can Coexist:** Balance a positive mindset with authenticity. Maintain hope while also permitting yourself to experience the full range of emotions.
7. **Your Story Has Power:** Sharing your journey can inspire others and bring healing to yourself. Vulnerability can be a gift for you and those who hear your story.
8. **Gratitude Amid Adversity**: Finding moments of thankfulness in the midst of struggle can shift your perspective and bring peace. Gratitude can coexist with pain and help you grow.

A JOURNEY OF FAITH, STRENGTH, AND HOPE

REFLECTIONS

FROM DIAGNOSIS TO DETERMINATION:
MY JOURNEY OF SURVIVAL

By Vivia Haye

> *I couldn't give up—not now, not like this. I was going to fight, not just for myself, but for my family, for my daughter who needed her mother, and for my brothers and sisters.*

My cancer journey began in the summer of 2021, just months after achieving a milestone I had worked tirelessly for—my doctoral degree. The sense of accomplishment was short-lived, as life soon threw me into a slippery slope of challenges. I was not only adjusting to a new job but also the daunting transition from academic life to the professional world. Amidst the chaos, I prioritized my health, scheduling routine checkups and a mammogram. I was proactive and determined to take control of my well-being.

When they found something suspicious, I felt a twinge of unease but dismissed it. "It's probably nothing," I thought. But when the biopsy results confirmed I had breast cancer, my world stopped. I was in shock. How could this be happening to me? I had always been mindful of my health—eating right, staying active, and doing everything I thought was necessary to prevent such a diagnosis. The news shattered the fragile sense of security I had built around my health. The oncologist explained that my cancer wasn't genetic; it was environmental, with stress playing a significant role. I felt betrayed by my own body, by life itself.

Breaking the news to my family was one of the hardest things I've ever had to do. My heart was heavy with a pain I could barely contain. The first person I told was my daughter. I remember holding her hand tightly, trying to steady my voice, but as soon as I saw the fear in her eyes, I broke down. We held each other, sobbing, clinging to the promise that we would get through this together. She was my strength at that moment, whispering reassurances through her tears, her words a fragile lifeline I desperately clung to.

Telling my siblings was another story. My eldest brother was already fighting his own battle with lymphoma, and I had been by his side, advocating fiercely for his care. How could I burden them with my illness when they were already carrying so much? I couldn't do it. I couldn't find the words, and before I could summon the courage, my brother passed away, never knowing that I, too, was fighting cancer. The guilt was suffocating. I felt like I had failed him, failed my family, and the weight of that grief was almost unbearable.

Chemotherapy was a trial that pushed me to the brink of my endurance. My body, once a vessel of strength, became unrecognizable to me. I watched as clumps of my hair fell away, leaving me feeling exposed and vulnerable. I lost weight, I lost strength, and, at times, I lost hope. I remember one particularly harrowing day when I was too weak to even keep water down. My nurse, seeing the defeat in my eyes, looked at me sternly and said, "Do you want to be a statistic, or are you going to fight?" Her words were like a slap to my soul, waking me from a daze of despair. I had a choice to make, and though it felt impossible, I chose to fight.

There were nights when the pain and nausea were so overwhelming that I was ready to let go, ready to say my goodbyes and give in to the darkness that loomed over me. I vividly remember the night of my brother's funeral. I was too weak to stand on my own, my hair gone, my body frail. People could see that I wasn't well, but it wasn't just grief that had taken its toll; it was the cancer that had invaded my body, my life.

After everyone had left that night, I lay in bed, feeling utterly broken. The sickness came in waves, relentless and unforgiving. One of my other brothers, a pastor, sat beside me and prayed. His words were filled with conviction, and he told me, "Sis, the Lord says He will heal you, but you have to fight with all you've got." At that moment, something inside me shifted. I felt a spark of determination reignite within me. I couldn't give up—not now, not like this. I was going to fight, not just for myself, but for my family, for my daughter who needed her mother, and for my brothers and sister who had already lost so much.

The road to recovery was long and arduous. Six grueling months of chemotherapy, followed by surgery, left me exhausted and scarred both physically and emotionally. It took another three months before I started feeling like myself again, and even then, it was a new version of myself, a woman forever changed by the battle I had endured. Physical therapy helped me regain the use of my hands, and slowly, I began to reconnect with the life I had once taken for granted.

Throughout it all, my faith was my anchor. I decluttered my life, letting go of everything that didn't serve me. I turned to prayer, even when the words wouldn't come, and I leaned on my prayer partner who called me every morning, her faith carrying me when I was too weak to carry myself. Over time, I felt a sense of peace settle over me, a quiet strength from knowing I was not alone in this fight. My connection with God deepened, and this faith, this unshakeable belief in something greater than myself, helped me survive.

As a nurse, my experience has profoundly changed how I view patient care. I've been on the other side of that bed, feeling the fear and the pain, and it has taught me that true empathy goes beyond understanding a diagnosis. It's about being in the trenches with someone, feeling their pain, hope, and despair. I teach my students to slow down, see the person behind the illness, and care with their whole hearts.

My cancer journey was a test of my spirit, my faith, and my will to live. It was a journey I wouldn't wish on anyone, but it has shaped me in ways I never imagined. It taught me the value of life, the power of faith, and the importance of human connection. And for that, I am eternally grateful.

DECLUTTERING

1. **Recognize Divine Record-Keeping**

In Vivia's case, her cancer diagnosis led to an unexpected moment of reflection. As someone who had lived healthily and believed in taking care of her body, her diagnosis felt contradictory. Vivia initially struggled to understand how she, a vegetarian who exercised regularly, could have developed cancer. It wasn't until later that she realized how stress had contributed to her illness. This realization mirrors the idea that God, not humans, keeps an accurate record of our lives. Vivia's journey reminded her that God's omniscient view encompassed factors beyond her understanding, even though she couldn't control or foresee certain outcomes. Vivia realized that her life is not under our complete control—even the healthiest habits can't fully protect us from suffering. God's plan and perspective include unseen variables that remind us of our limitations and need for divine trust.

2. **Embrace God's Perspective**

As Vivia reflected on her situation, she came to terms with the fact that God had a broader understanding of her life, health, and circumstances. She accepted that there were factors beyond her control, such as environmental influences, and her battle with cancer was part of a larger divine narrative. This acceptance of God's perspective allowed her to reframe her suffering in a spiritual context, deepening her faith and providing her with the strength to continue fighting. Vivia learned that trusting God's understanding of your life can provide peace and resilience when faced with uncertainties.

3. **Heavenly Judgment**

Vivia acknowledged that her struggle was not only physical but spiritual, and the outcomes of her life were ultimately in God's hands, not judged by human standards. Her experience in the hospital, where she was forced to advocate for herself and rely on God's mercy, reinforced the idea that the battles we face in life have divine significance beyond what we can comprehend. Understanding that life's struggles are part of a spiritual test encourages cancer survivors to see their battles as part of a greater divine purpose. Knowing that God sees and judges our lives beyond human understanding provides peace.

4. **Accept Divine Sacrifice**

A turning point in Vivia's journey occurred when her brother, a pastor, prayed with her and reminded her that God would heal her if she fought with all her strength. This moment was a profound spiritual awakening for Vivia, leading her to embrace the sacrifice and grace offered by God. By choosing to fight through her illness, she accepted that her strength and healing came from God, not just from herself. Relying on God's sacrifice for healing underscores the importance of faith in overcoming a graven illness.

5. **Acknowledge and Reject Wrongdoings**

During her cancer journey, Vivia experienced a period of introspection and decluttering—both physically and spiritually. She realized that stress had played a significant role in her illness and that there were aspects of her life she needed to let go of. Her reflection led her to reevaluate what was important and reject any aspects of her life that did not serve her well-being or spiritual health. Spiritual decluttering involves acknowledging and releasing unhealthy attachments—whether it's emotional baggage or stress—that contribute to illness.

6. **Reconciliation in Christ**

Vivia's connection with God grew stronger as she went through her treatments and recovery. She recognized that her battle with cancer was not hers alone but something that she could face with God's strength. Her reconciliation with Christ was evident in her prayers, reliance on faith, and ability to embrace hope despite her suffering. Reconciliation with God brings peace and resilience to those facing terminal illness. Vivia's experience encourages survivors to deepen their spiritual connection, allowing them to face their journey with faith and trust in divine grace.

7. **Certainty of Eternal Life**

Vivia had fully embraced the certainty of eternal life and viewed her illness as part of a larger spiritual test. Her faith in God's promises gave her hope, even when her body was physically weakened. Vivia's story illustrates that certainty in eternal life can help survivors shift their focus from fear of death to appreciating life's spiritual lessons. Finding hope in eternal life can transform the fear and uncertainty of a terminal illness into a spiritual journey. Vivia's acceptance of eternal life gave her a renewed perspective, helping her focus on what truly mattered—faith, family, and God's love.

Major Takeaways for Other Cancer Survivors:

1. **Faith Over Fear:** Embracing faith can provide strength, hope, and peace during a terminal illness.
2. **Embrace the Unseen Variables:** Trust in a higher plan and let go of the need to control every outcome.
3. **Self-Advocacy with Divine Help:** Advocate for your health while recognizing the role of divine intervention in your healing.
4. **Support Systems Are Crucial:** Seek and embrace strong spiritual and emotional support systems.
5. **Hope in Eternal Life:** Focus on the certainty of eternal life to transform fear of death into peace and acceptance.

MY JOURNEY OF SURVIVAL

REFLECTIONS

NAVIGATING LIFE'S STORMS: FROM CHILDHOOD STRUGGLES TO CANCER SURVIVAL

By Ariane Navarro

Pouring my pain, my anger, my confusion onto the page helped me make sense of the chaos inside me.

Growing up in the busy city of Houston, Texas, I learned early on what it meant to survive in a world that constantly tested my strength. My parents divorced when I was just five years old, leaving my mother to raise me and my siblings in a crowded home that never seemed to quiet down. We were crammed into a house overflowing with family members, all vying for space, privacy, and a moment of peace. It was like living in a pressure cooker—conflict was inevitable, and I became adept at navigating the tumultuous waters of clashing personalities and simmering tensions. I had no choice but to adapt, to find ways to protect myself from the noise and the emotional turmoil that swirled around me.

Yet, amidst the chaos, there was a moment that shattered my young world more profoundly than any argument or family drama ever could. I was just ten years old when I experienced my first panic attack—a terror that seized me so completely I could barely breathe. Not long after, overwhelmed by a darkness I couldn't understand, I tried to end my life by swallowing a handful of pills. My memories from that time are fragmented, a blur of fear and confusion. But there is one thing I remember with heartbreaking clarity—my mother saving my life. Instead of dismissing my actions as something that could be prayed away, she took me to a psychiatrist, a decision that would shape my future in ways neither of us could have foreseen.

I spent two weeks in a psychiatric hospital, a place where the innocence of childhood was starkly contrasted with the harsh realities of abuse, trauma, and fear that other children faced. It was a world that terrified me, and yet, it was there that a seed was planted—a seed that would one day grow into a deep commitment to understanding mental health and the invisible battles so many of us fight.

Years later, just as I was beginning to carve out a life for myself as a bilingual kindergarten teacher, married with a five-year-old son, that darkness came for me again, this time in the form of a cancer diagnosis. I was 26, full of hope and plans for the future, when I heard the word "leukemia" fall from the doctor's lips. I fell into a dark abyss. I remember the look on my husband's face, the tears he tried so hard to hold back, and the shock that turned my mother's face pale. How was this possible?

I had just begun to build my life, and now it felt like it was crumbling before my eyes.

But I went into survival mode. With a young child depending on me, I didn't have the luxury of staying down. I had to be strong; I had to climb out, not just for myself but for my family. I moved through the days in a haze, more machine than human. I was relentless in my determination to live, focusing on work, navigating the labyrinth of insurance, and enduring grueling treatments that left me feeling hollow and numb. I couldn't let fear consume me; I couldn't afford to feel the weight of my despair.

And then, just as I thought I was finding my footing again, I relapsed. It was three months after I had given birth to my second son—a moment that should have been filled with joy and hope. Instead, it became the beginning of another nightmare. The cancer was back, more aggressive than before, and this time, it brought with it a despair so deep it nearly swallowed me whole. I had done everything right. I had followed the treatments, endured the pain, fought with every ounce of strength I had, and still, it wasn't enough. The treatments were harsher, the hospital stays longer, and I felt my spirit crumbling under the weight of it all.

I was angry. I was angry at God for what felt like a betrayal, angry at the world for moving on as if nothing had happened, and angry at myself for not being stronger. I felt like I was drowning, and no matter how hard I tried to swim, the current kept pulling me under. People don't tell you about the emotional aftermath of surviving cancer, the way it haunts you, the way it steals your peace even when the doctors say you're in remission. I fell into a deep depression, numbing myself with pain medications that couldn't touch the anguish in my soul. I overdosed more times than I care to admit, lost in a fog of despair that seemed inescapable.

The turning point came in the most unexpected and heartbreaking way. I had decided that my family would be better off without me, that my boys would be spared the pain of watching their mother suffer. I turned on the car in the garage, falsely content, ready to let go of the fight. And then, during that dark moment, a thought pierced through the fog. My son was waiting for me to pick him up from school. I saw his little face in my mind, full of trust and love, and I knew I couldn't do it. I couldn't leave him with the trauma of losing his mother this way. That realization hit me like a lightning bolt, pulling me back from the brink.

It wasn't an instant transformation. Recovery is never a straight line, and mine was no exception. But that moment was the start of something new, a tiny spark of hope amid overwhelming darkness. I turned to writing, something I had done since childhood. Pouring my pain, anger, and confusion onto the page helped me make sense of the chaos inside me. It was through writing that I began to see my strength and resilience. I started to believe that maybe, just maybe, I could survive this too.

Today, I am committed to advocacy and sharing my story so that others battling their demons know they are not alone. I work with cancer organizations, focusing on young adult survivors and advocating for mental health support in underserved communities. It's a mission that has become my lifeline, a way to turn my pain into purpose. I want people to know that surviving cancer is about more than just beating the disease—it's about finding the strength to rebuild your life, piece by broken piece.

Cancer took so much from me, but it also gave me clarity. It forced me to examine my life and see what truly mattered. I learned to set boundaries, say no, and create a space of love and safety for myself and my family. I've built a life that reflects the stability and peace I longed for as a child. And that, more than anything, is my greatest victory.

DECLUTTERING

1. **Recognize Divine Record-Keeping:**

Ariane's journey begins with a deep connection to her faith, particularly in the early stages of her life. She was raised in a religious environment that influenced her understanding of life, illness, and struggle. However, when she faced the recurrence of cancer, her belief in this framework was deeply challenged. She expressed anger and questioned why God allowed her to suffer again after having already survived once. This is a key part of recognizing divine record-keeping—understanding that every action and thought is part of a larger, divine record, even when it feels like suffering doesn't make sense. Ariane's struggle with this realization reflects her spiritual battle, where she might learn to accept that God's view may include elements she cannot yet see.

2. **Embrace God's Perspective:**

Ariane's experience with spiritual decluttering begins when she questions her religious upbringing. Initially, she felt comforted by her faith, but with her relapse, her worldview shifted. She had done everything "right" in her mind, yet her cancer returned. This step challenges her to embrace a broader, more universal understanding of God's plan. By acknowledging that God's perspective encompasses all of human nature, not just her pain, Ariane begins to shift from anger and confusion to an understanding that suffering might have a deeper purpose, one that she cannot fully grasp.

3. **Heavenly Judgment:**

Ariane's story reflects the struggle between human and divine judgment. Throughout her cancer journey, she felt the weight of others' judgment when they would offer toxic positivity, saying things like "God only gives his toughest battles to His strongest soldiers." Ariane's anger toward this kind of judgment reveals her journey toward accepting that ultimate judgment belongs to God, not humans. This step helps her recognize that her worth and the meaning of her suffering are not determined by others' perceptions but by a higher, divine purpose.

4. **Accept Divine Sacrifice:**

As Ariane navigates her illness and her subsequent mental health struggles, her faith in divine sacrifice becomes shaky. She is angry with God for what feels like betrayal. However, her eventual shift toward healing reflects her acceptance of the possibility of God's greater plan for her life, even if she cannot fully understand it in the moment.

5. **Acknowledge and Reject Wrongdoings:**

Ariane's acknowledgment of her struggles, including her overdoses and moments of mental health crises, aligns with this step of spiritual decluttering. She does not shy away from accepting her wrongdoings, even when faced with judgment from others who cannot understand her battle with depression and addiction. Her openness about these moments and her recognition that they were part of a larger emotional response to her illness allows her to reject the darker version of herself that almost gave in to despair.

6. **Reconciliation in Christ:**

Ariane's story of redemption truly begins when she acknowledges her role as a mother and wife. Her turning point comes when she decides not to end her life because of the impact it would have on her son. This moment is key in her reconciliation, as she recognizes that God has not abandoned her, and instead, she has the opportunity to rebuild her life with her family. Reconciliation is also evident in her new outlook, as she begins to focus on her advocacy for other survivors and her mission to help underserved communities navigate the emotional and physical aftermath of cancer. Her reconciliation is ongoing, but it is clear that through Christ, she is healing and finding a new sense of purpose.

7. **Certainty of Eternal Life:**

Ariane's journey reflects the slow but steady realization that life, including its most painful moments, is part of a larger, eternal narrative. Though she battles with doubt, despair, and loss, she ultimately embraces the idea that her suffering has meaning beyond the here and now. Her work with cancer survivors, her advocacy for mental health, and her commitment to writing a memoir reflect her newfound understanding of eternal life. This understanding helps her reframe her cancer journey, not as something that defines her negatively but as something that prepares her for eternal peace and helps her find purpose in the present.

Major Takeaways for Other Cancer Survivors

1. **It's Okay to Question Faith:** Doubts, anger, and questioning God's plan are natural responses to suffering, and these emotions can ultimately lead to a stronger, more personal faith.
2. **You Are More Than Your Illness:** Cancer survivors can find purpose beyond their diagnosis by recognizing their strengths, talents, and contributions.
3. **Mental Health is Key:** Acknowledging mental health challenges and seeking help is crucial. It's okay to experience depression, anxiety, and even moments of hopelessness as long as you find ways to heal.
4. **Community Matters:** Finding a supportive community that allows for authentic emotions rather than forcing positivity, is essential for emotional recovery.
5. **Redefining Success:** Life after cancer may look different, but that doesn't diminish its value. Survivors can find new meaning in their experiences, turning them into opportunities for growth and advocacy.

FROM CHILDHOOD STRUGGLES TO CANCER SURVIVAL

REFLECTIONS

VICTORY IS MINE:
A TEST OF FAITH, LOVE, AND STRENGTH

By Charmaine Hudson

As I stand on the other side of this battle, I see that cancer didn't defeat me. It transformed me.

L ife can change instantly with a single phone call, and suddenly, you're facing your worst fear. My name is Charmaine, and my story is about walking through the valley of fear and doubt only to discover that love, faith, and resilience can see you through anything—even breast cancer.

I grew up on the island of St. Lucia, raised by a single mother who was a rock of faith. We didn't have much, but we made up for what we lacked in material wealth with love and a deep connection to God. Every Saturday, without fail, my sisters and I would dress in our best clothes and walk to church with my mother. Church wasn't just a place we went; it was where we learned to trust God with everything. Little did I know those early morning walks to church would build the foundation for the faith I would need in the years to come.

In my early 20s, I left St. Lucia and moved to the United States, driven by dreams of furthering my nursing career. I landed in Huntsville, Alabama, where I juggled two schools to get my nursing degree. It was overwhelming, and I found myself often on my knees, begging God for strength. I remember one night, after hours of studying, I broke down. God, I can't do this without You. I opened my Bible, desperate for an answer, and my eyes fell on Proverbs 3:5, "Trust in the Lord with all your heart and lean not on your own understanding." It felt like a lifeline, pulling me out of the storm. From that moment on, I knew God had a plan for me, and I held on to that faith through every hardship.

It was also in Huntsville that I met my husband. He was from St. Lucia, too, and we shared the same values, faith, and deep love for family. We got married in 1999, full of hope for the future. I had my nursing career and a beautiful marriage, and soon, we were blessed with a daughter, Abigail, who became the light of our lives.

But life doesn't always follow the path we expect. Two years into our marriage, I discovered a couple of lumps in my breast. Fear prickled at the edges of my mind, but the doctors assured me they were benign cysts. For nearly 20 years, I lived with this cloud of uncertainty over my head, but every mammogram came back clear. I stopped worrying. I had my faith, family, and health—or so I thought.

Then, everything changed. In my 50s, one of the lumps started to grow. It was my husband who noticed it first. "Baby, what's this?" he asked, gently touching the swollen area. My heart sank, but I still held onto hope. "It's probably nothing," I told myself. "It's just another cyst." But when I found another lump under my arm, I knew something was wrong.

We were on a family vacation in Orlando when I got the mammogram that changed my life. I still remember the sterile smell of the doctor's office and the cold weight of the words as they hit me: "Charmaine, you have stage three breast cancer." Everything inside me collapsed. Stage three? How many stages are there? Four? My God, I'm almost at the end. I could hear my heartbeat in my ears as I walked out of the hospital, trying to breathe, trying to hold myself together.

I called my husband first. His voice was calm and steady as if he knew exactly what I needed. "Baby, how many stages are there?" he asked. "Four," I whispered, my throat tight with fear. "Then we're not done yet," he said with a strength that brought me back from the brink. "We're going to fight this. We'll get through this together."

But the road ahead was terrifying. I had to start chemotherapy, and the side effects were immediate. The nausea, the fatigue, the relentless toll on my body—it felt like I was being poisoned from the inside out. And then, the hair loss. It was like losing a part of myself. My identity, my femininity—everything that I thought made me "me" was disappearing. I stood there, staring at my reflection, feeling utterly broken.

I was afraid of how my husband would see me. I didn't want him to look at me and see the sickness, the ugliness I felt inside.

One night, in a moment of vulnerability, I told him, "I don't have hair. I don't have breasts. I don't even have my uterus anymore. What's left of me?" I'll never forget what he said next. "Baby, I didn't marry your hair. I didn't marry your breasts. I married you." I crumbled in his arms. At that moment, I knew I wasn't alone in this fight. He loved me—even in the midst of my struggle.

But my husband wasn't my only support. At 86 years old, my mother was by my side every day. Even when I was too sick to eat, she would gently ask, "Charmaine, what can I make you? Just tell me, and I'll cook it." My sisters took turns flying in from all over to care for me, massaging my feet every night before bed. And my daughter, Abigail—my precious girl—made it her mission to make me laugh every day. After school, she'd sit beside me with jokes, silly stories, anything to bring a smile to my face. In those moments, surrounded by their love, I felt hope, even when my body was screaming at me to give up.

Through it all, I clung to my faith. I surrounded myself with scripture, prayers, and the belief that God had a plan for me, even in this. There were days when I couldn't understand why this was happening. I remember one day, driving alone in my car, tears streaming down my face, and instead of asking, "Why me?" I found myself saying, "Thank You, God, for this journey." It didn't make sense, but somehow, deep down, I knew this was a path I had to walk. And even in the pain, I felt His presence, guiding me, holding me.

Chemotherapy, surgery, radiation—it all felt like a never-ending nightmare. I had a double mastectomy, and because of the BRCA gene, I also had to have a hysterectomy. Everything that made me feel like a woman was taken from me. But something incredible happened in the midst of that loss. My spirit, my faith, and my love for my family grew stronger than ever. My husband would look at me, his eyes full of love, and tell me I was beautiful, even when I felt like a shadow of my former self. Slowly, I started to believe him.

My work, family, friends, and church were there for me every step of the way. My colleagues sent me gifts—one for every recovery day after surgery. My friends prayed for me, fasted for me, and held me up when I was too weak to stand. And through it all, I felt God's love in every act of kindness, every prayer whispered in my name.

Now, as I stand on the other side of this battle, I see that cancer didn't defeat me. It transformed me. It stripped away everything superficial and left me with a deeper connection to God, a stronger bond with my family, and an unshakable faith. I no longer fear what the future holds because I know whatever happens, God is with me.

I used to think my story was about surviving cancer, but now I know it's about so much more. It's about the power of love—love from my husband, family, friends, and most of all, God. Cancer may have taken parts of my body, but it gave me something far greater: the knowledge that I am loved beyond measure and that, no matter what, I will never walk this journey alone.

DECLUTTERING

1. **Recognize Divine Record-Keeping:**

In the midst of her cancer diagnosis, Charmaine's life seemed to unravel. But in the uncertainty, she instinctively recognized that it was not human hands that held her fate but God's. This understanding was clear when she opened her Bible to Proverbs 3:5, "Trust in the Lord with all your heart and lean not on your own understanding." This marked a pivotal moment where Charmaine began to see her cancer not as a random tragedy but as part of a divine plan—one that only God fully understood. She knew He saw and recorded every tear, every prayer, and every fear.

Her journey was not just physical but deeply spiritual. Charmaine embraced that God was watching over her, witnessing her pain, strength, and moments of weakness. She trusted that He was keeping a record, not of her suffering alone, but of her faithfulness during the suffering. Recognizing this gave her the strength to endure the uncertainty that came with every treatment and every diagnosis.

2. Embrace God's Perspective:

Her mother's steadfast belief in God shaped Charmaine's faith journey from an early age. Even though she had lived a life of devotion, cancer forced her to look beyond her human understanding and see things from God's perspective. She realized that her suffering was not a punishment but a part of the larger story God was telling through her life.

When her husband reassured her, saying, "We're not done yet," Charmaine began to see her battle with cancer through a divine lens. She understood that God was aware of her suffering and used this experience to deepen her trust in Him. Charmaine embraced the idea that God's perspective was infinite, while her own was limited by human fear and doubt. By seeing her illness through God's eyes, she found peace knowing that her suffering had a purpose.

3. **Heavenly Judgment:**

At the moment of diagnosis, Charmaine's immediate fear was of earthly consequences. "I'm going to die," she thought. But as she progressed through her treatment, she came to understand that her life was not being judged by earthly standards but by heavenly ones. She recognized that her faith, her relationship with God, and her love for her family were what truly mattered in the grand scheme of things.

This realization helped her shift her focus from fear of physical death to the assurance of spiritual life. She was no longer afraid of the judgment that might come from her illness or from the physical changes she endured. Her true worth, she understood, was measured not by her health or appearance but by her faithfulness to God. She accepted that God's judgment was one of grace and love, not condemnation.

4. **Accept Divine Sacrifice:**

In her most vulnerable moments, when Charmaine was stripped of her hair, her breasts, and even her uterus, she came face to face with the reality of her frailty. In these moments, she fully embraced God's divine sacrifice on her behalf. The love and support she received from her husband, her family, and her friends mirrored the unconditional love of Christ, reminding her that she was cherished not for her physical body but for her soul.

Charmaine knew that Jesus had already endured the ultimate suffering on the cross, and because of His sacrifice, she didn't have to walk through her cancer journey alone. When she prayed and felt God's presence, she realized that His sacrifice was not just for her salvation but for her strength in moments like these. She accepted that through Christ's death, she was given the strength to endure the suffering of her illness and the hope of eternal life.

5. Acknowledge and Reject Wrongdoings:

Throughout her life, Charmaine had been committed to living a faithful, righteous life. But as she faced the reality of her cancer, she was forced to confront the parts of herself that harbored fear and doubt. It was not that she had done wrong by contracting cancer, but she had to battle the internal voices that questioned her worth in the face of her illness. The fear of being unloved because of her changed body, the worry that her illness might be a form of divine punishment—all of these thoughts weighed on her.

However, she consciously rejected these fears and doubts. With every prayer and every affirmation of faith, Charmaine chose to reject the undesired version of herself that was consumed by fear. She refused to let cancer define her or dictate her relationship with God. Instead, she embraced the truth of who she was—a beloved child of God, deserving of His love and mercy.

6. Reconciliation in Christ:

One of the most beautiful aspects of Charmaine's story is how she reconciled her suffering with her faith. Rather than seeing her illness as a curse, she came to see it as an opportunity for deeper communion with Christ. She experienced moments of overwhelming peace, even in the midst of her physical suffering, as if God was holding her hand through every trial.

When Charmaine thanked God for the journey, even while sobbing in her car, it was a profound moment of reconciliation. She had come to terms with the reality of her illness and had made peace with it through her relationship with Christ. She no longer saw herself as a victim of cancer but as a victor through Christ, reconciled to the truth that her life, no matter its length, was in God's hands.

7. **Certainty of Eternal Life:**

The final step in spiritual decluttering is the acceptance of eternal life, a constant theme in Charmaine's story. From the beginning, her faith had taught her that this life was temporary and her ultimate goal was to spend eternity with God. Even in the face of a terminal illness, Charmaine found peace in knowing that death was not the end but merely a transition into eternal life with Christ.

Her faith in eternal life gave her the courage to face the possibility of death without fear. As she said, "If I were to die, I would still be happy because I'm dying in Him, with Him." This certainty allowed her to face the challenges of cancer with a strength that can only come from knowing that this life is not all there is. It gave her hope for healing in this life and the eternal healing that comes through Christ.

Major Takeaways for Other Cancer Survivors

1. **Faith as an Anchor:** In times of crisis, faith can provide strength and stability.
2. **Embrace Vulnerability:** It's okay to feel scared and weak; what's important is to keep moving forward.

3. **Surround Yourself with Love:** The support of loved ones can make a significant difference.
4. **Power in Letting Go:** Accepting what you can't control and accepting God's providence can bring peace.
5. **Hope Over Fear:** Hope can be a powerful motivator, even in the face of fear.
6. **Unique Journey:** Everyone's journey is different; trust God to help you navigate it.
7. **Find Peace in Uncertainty:** Trust that you are not alone; God is with you even in uncertain times.

A TEST OF FAITH, LOVE, AND STRENGTH

REFLECTIONS

SILENT WARRIOR:
A JOURNEY FROM SURVIVAL TO ADVOCACY

By Jade Gibson

I am a survivor, yes, but I am also so much more.
I am an advocate, a fighter, someone who refuses to be silenced.

I was just 16 years old when my entire world was turned upside down. Growing up in Macon, Georgia, as an only child, it was just my mom and me. We were a team, navigating life's ups and downs together. My mom worked tirelessly in the manufacturing industry, sacrificing much to provide for us. She was my rock, and I was her quiet, shy daughter who didn't have many friends. I spent most of my teenage years working at a wig boutique, watching people come and go, many of them cancer patients, but never imagining that one day I would be one of them.

It all started with something so seemingly small—irregular menstrual cycles. I was just 15, and my mom, always vigilant, took me to see a gynecologist. He said the doctor found what he believed was a harmless cyst, something "normal" for girls my age. So we didn't worry too much. But deep down, I felt something wasn't right.

Months passed, and my symptoms grew worse—nausea, fatigue, and a constant, uncomfortable bloating in my abdomen. I went to the ER, urgent care, and my primary doctor multiple times, but no one took me seriously. It felt like I was screaming into a void, my cries for help disappearing into the wind. They told me it was just menstrual-related and that I was fine. But I knew something was terribly wrong. It was like a shadow looming over me, growing darker each day.

It wasn't until six months later, when we went back to the gynecologist that the seriousness of my condition was finally acknowledged. This time, they did more tests and imaging, and the truth came crashing down on us like a tidal wave—stage 3 ovarian cancer. My mom received the call, but she didn't tell me right away. She waited until the school year ended, sparing me from the devastating news until I finished my sophomore year.

When she finally told me, I felt like I was in a nightmare. Cancer. It was a word I had heard so many times, a word associated with the people I saw at the boutique, the women who came in looking for wigs to cover their bald heads, their faces lined with pain and hope. But now, it was my reality. My summer plans, like those of any other teenager, were replaced with a grueling schedule of surgeries and treatments.

The surgery was brutal. I had metal staples in my abdomen, and every movement was agony. I remember lying in bed, trying not to breathe too deeply because even that hurt. Laughing, crying, even just existing felt like a battle against my own body. My family treated me like I was made of glass, and in many ways, I was. I felt fragile, broken, like a porcelain doll on the verge of shattering.

And then came the chemotherapy. Eight rounds of poison pumped into my veins, each one stripping away a part of me. The first round wasn't so bad—I remember thinking, "I can do this." But as the treatments continued, the reality set in. It was nausea so intense it felt like I was being ripped apart from the inside, vomiting until I was too weak to cry, and the hair loss. My hair fell out in clumps, and with each strand that fell, I felt like I was losing a piece of myself. My mom took it harder than I did. She watched as her little girl, her baby, became someone unrecognizable. She tried to be strong, but I could see the pain in her eyes every time she looked at me.

As I fought through the treatments, questions swirled in my mind—questions about my future, my fertility, and whether I would ever get to be a mother. I was only 16, but the weight of these questions pressed down on me like a thousand-pound weight. The doctors couldn't give me answers. They told me they wouldn't know the full extent of the damage until they opened me up. I was terrified.

After surgery, I lost one ovary and one fallopian tube. It was like a piece of my womanhood had been ripped away. But there was still hope. I clung to that hope like a lifeline through every round of chemo, through every moment when I thought

I couldn't go on. I dropped to 98 pounds, my body emaciated, my spirit hanging on by a thread. But I kept going for myself, my mom, and everyone who believed in me.

After the treatments ended, everyone expected me to just go back to being "normal" to pick up where I left off. But how could I? I had missed my entire junior year of high school. I had to take extra courses just to graduate on time. But more than that, I had missed being a teenager. Cancer had stolen so much from me—my innocence, my carefree days, my sense of normalcy. I was left feeling lost, like a stranger in my own life.

There was no mental health support, no one to help me navigate the emotional wreckage cancer had left behind. I felt silenced like my voice didn't matter, like my pain wasn't real because the cancer was gone. But the scars were still there, invisible but so very real. It took years for me to find my voice again and feel like I had a right to speak and be heard.

Now, I use that voice to advocate for others. I fight for young adults with rare diseases, helping them access the resources they need and the support they deserve. I work to ensure that no one else has to go through what I did alone and unheard. I want to make sure that every young person facing this monster has someone in their corner, fighting for them and believing in them.

Cancer changed me, but it didn't break me. It forged me in fire and turned my pain into purpose. I am a survivor, yes, but I am also so much more. I am an advocate, a fighter, someone who refuses to be silenced. My journey has been hard, filled with moments of darkness and despair. But it has also been a journey of strength, resilience, and finding hope in the most unexpected places.

So, I keep fighting, using my voice, and helping others find theirs. No one should have to walk this path alone, and if my story can help even one person feel less alone, it has all been worth it.

USE JADE'S STORY TO PRACTICE DECLUTTERING
Major Takeaways for Young Adult Cancer Survivors

1. **Advocate for Yourself:** Trust your instincts and be persistent when something feels wrong. Don't be afraid to ask questions and seek second opinions, even if it feels like your concerns are being dismissed.
2. **Mental Health Matters:** Physical recovery is just one part of the journey. Pay attention to your mental health and seek support when needed. It's okay to feel overwhelmed, and asking for help is a sign of strength, not weakness.
3. **Build a Support Network:** Whether it's family, friends, or healthcare professionals, having people you trust to support you during and after treatment is essential. Lean on them when things get tough.
4. **Understand Your Body:** You are the expert of your own body. Keep track of symptoms, changes, and how you feel. Don't hesitate to speak up when something seems off, even post-treatment.
5. **There is No "Normal" After Cancer:** Life after cancer is a new chapter, but it doesn't have to look like what it was before. Allow yourself time to adjust, focusing on what makes you feel fulfilled.

6. **Stay Informed About Resources:** Be proactive in seeking out resources for cancer survivors, whether it's financial assistance, educational support, or mental health services. Often, these resources exist but aren't always offered upfront.
7. **Find Purpose in Advocacy:** Sharing your story or supporting others can be a powerful way to heal and make a difference. Advocating for others helps raise awareness and improves the system for future patients.

A JOURNEY FROM SURVIVAL TO ADVOCACY

REFLECTIONS

CHOOSING LIFE:
A JOURNEY OF FAITH AND RESILIENCE

By Peter Campbell

I needed to stop consuming death and start choosing life.

I was born under the warm Bahamian sun, surrounded by the endless blue of the Caribbean Sea, and raised across the islands of Jamaica and the Cayman Islands—a true child of the tropics. My father was a pastor, and his calling took us to different corners of the world as the church needed. My parents had settled in Jamaica, but when my mother's doctor advised her to return to the Bahamas for my birth, she did. It turned out to be the same for my brother and sister. We would all be born in the Bahamas, even though Jamaica was home. Growing up in the 1970s in the Caribbean was like living in a dream. I remember our first home in the Cayman Islands, a little house right on the beach. We'd step out of the back door and into the sand, the ocean stretching out before us like a beautiful promise. Early mornings were filled with the laughter of our neighbors snorkeling in the crystal-clear waters, keeping a watchful eye on us kids as we played in the waves. It was a childhood painted in hues of sunshine, warm sands, and the comforting lullaby of the sea.

But life, as it often does, took a turn. My father received a call to further his studies at the seminary at Andrews University in Michigan. It was his pathway to serving in church conferences in the United States. I was just a child when we moved, and the transition was a shock that reverberated through my little world. We went from the sun-kissed beaches of the Caribbean to the bone-chilling cold of Michigan. I remember the first time I felt snow beneath my feet, the way the cold bit through my skin, and the sky seemed to hang low and gray. It was more than just a physical shock—it was a cultural one, too. Everything was different. But kids are resilient, and I adapted, finding my place in this strange new world.

After my father completed his Master of Divinity in just one year, we moved to Salisbury, Maryland. It was there that we started to truly put down roots. Salisbury was a place of warmth, not just from the sun but from the community that embraced us. My father pastored three churches, and I found a sense of belonging amidst the vibrant Black community. I made friends who are still a part of my life today—those years shaped me profoundly, teaching me the strength of community, the power of faith, and the importance of resilience.

My father's ministry was a central part of my life. He was not just a good preacher—he was a beacon of hope, an anchor in the ever-shifting tides of our lives. I was baptized at eight years old, but it wasn't until I was older that I truly understood what it meant to have a relationship with God. My father's office door was always open, and I could ask him anything about faith, scripture, or life. Unlike many pastor's kids who feel crushed by expectations, I was blessed. My parents cultivated genuine friendships with church members, and we were treated with kindness and respect. It was a testament to the love and care my parents showed to everyone they met.

But my faith, though rooted deeply in my upbringing, was tested in ways I could never have imagined. In September of 2022, my world was turned upside down when I was diagnosed with stage four colon cancer that had spread to my liver and lungs. I had been feeling unwell for a while, dismissing the symptoms as something minor, like IBS. But after several tests and an emergency room visit, the truth hit like a sledgehammer. I was in the hospital when the ER doctor delivered the news. I remember the moment vividly. As she approached my room, I felt a strange sensation, like a gentle breeze washing over me, and I heard the words, "Relax, don't worry." It was as if God Himself was speaking to me, wrapping me in a blanket of calm amidst the chaos. I wasn't afraid. I wasn't shattered. I was at peace because I knew that whatever happened was part of His plan.

I began chemotherapy in March 2023, a journey that would last over a year, stretching into July 2024. The treatments were brutal, each session leaving me feeling like I was being torn apart from the inside out. My hands turned dark, my nails almost black, and walking became a torment due to the neuropathy that gnawed at my feet. Each chemo drug brought its own set of horrors, but the worst was when swallowing even a sip of water felt like swallowing broken glass. I felt like I was being fed death in small doses, and I knew I had to make a change. One day, it hit me: I needed to stop consuming death and start choosing life. I turned to a diet of raw fruits, vegetables, and foods that would nourish my body instead of tearing it apart. It was my way of fighting back and taking control of my life in a situation where I felt powerless.

Despite the pain, despite the numbers not going in the direction I hoped, I held on to the promise I heard that night in the hospital. I told her, "Relax, don't worry." I opened up about my journey on social media, sharing the highs and lows, the moments of despair, and the glimmers of hope. I didn't want to hide my condition. I wanted people to know, to pray for me, to support me, and to stand with me in this battle.

Now, as I prepare to go to Eden Valley, a wellness center in Colorado that focuses on natural healing, I am filled with hope. I believe that the treatments there will help me reset and restore my body. This journey with cancer has taught me so much—about valuing life, about the power of honesty in the face of fear, and about drawing closer to God. My faith has grown stronger through this trial, and I've come to understand that no matter what happens, God is in control. He's whispering to all of us, "Relax, don't worry." And that's where I find my peace.

This journey has not been easy. It has been filled with moments of pain so intense it felt like I was drowning, moments when I questioned everything I believed. But through it all, I've held on to my faith, to the love of my family and friends, and to the belief that there is a purpose in this suffering. I don't know what the future holds, but I know who holds my future. And that, more than anything, gives me the strength to keep fighting, to keep believing, and to keep choosing life.

Major Takeaways for Other Cancer Survivors

1. **Embrace Faith and Positivity:** Hold on to faith and positivity to guide you through tough times. Trust that your pain has a purpose and believe in your spirit's strength.
2. **Listen to Your Body:** Pay attention to your body's signals. Advocate for yourself and seek timely medical advice if something feels off.
3. **Seek Support from Your Community:** Lean on your family, friends, and faith community for support. Their love and strength can help you through difficult moments.
4. **Consider Lifestyle and Diet Changes:** Choose nourishing foods that support your healing journey. Opt for raw fruits, vegetables, and whole foods to strengthen your body.
5. **Take Control of Your Treatment:** Be proactive in your treatment decisions. Explore all options and make choices that align with your values and beliefs.
6. **Focus on Quality of Life:** Prioritize treatments and decisions that enhance your quality of life. Aim to live well and find joy even amidst challenges.

7. **Stay Resilient and Flexible:** Be prepared for unexpected turns and remain adaptable. Resilience is about rising stronger after each fall.
8. **Cultivate Hope and Purpose:** Find something meaningful to hold on to, whether faith, family, or passions. Let these be your reasons to keep fighting.
9. **Value Every Moment:** Cherish time with loved ones and live in the present. Make memories and let each moment reflect your strength and courage.
10. **Don't Be Afraid to Ask for Help:** Even the strongest need support. Reach out for medical advice, emotional support, or just a shoulder to lean on. Asking for help is a sign of bravery, not weakness. You don't have to face this journey alone.

A JOURNEY OF FAITH AND RESILIENCE

REFLECTIONS

A NURSE'S JOURNEY:
ADVOCACY, CARE, AND THE FIGHT AGAINST CANCER

By Debra Rundles

I advocated for my patients, their dignity, and their right to be seen and heard.

More than 25 years ago, my life took a turn that I could never have anticipated, one that would shape not only my career but also my very soul. It all began with a patient named Miss Daisy, a dignified and graceful African American woman whose spirit touched me deeply. As a home health nurse, I was responsible for administering her medications, checking her vital signs, and coordinating her care. But the connection we built was much more than that. We shared stories, laughter, and moments of quiet understanding. Her strength and calm acceptance of life's challenges taught me lessons that no medical textbook ever could.

I still remember the day she told me she had been diagnosed with breast cancer. The air seemed to thicken with the weight of her words. My heart broke for her, but she remained serene as if she had already made peace with it. She looked me in the eyes and said, "I prayed to live long enough to see my youngest daughter graduate, and now that wish has come true. I won't bargain with God for more time." Her faith, her quiet strength, and her acceptance of what was to come—it all left me in awe.

At the time, I knew little about oncology, but I knew one thing for certain: I could not let her face this alone. I was there when she prepared for surgery, holding her hand as she faced the unknown with a courage that humbled me. She needed a new drug called tamoxifen for her treatment, but it wasn't covered by Medicaid or Medicare back then. I remember feeling a surge of anger and frustration. How could this be? How could the system fail someone as deserving as Miss Daisy?

Determined to help her, I reached out to the drug manufacturer, advocating on her behalf. I made phone calls, wrote letters, and refused to take no for an answer. And finally, we won. Miss Daisy received her medication at no cost. That moment changed everything for me. It was more than just a victory; it was a revelation. I realized that my role wasn't just about administering care—it was about fighting for my patients, standing in the gap for them, and navigating a healthcare system that often seemed more focused on barriers than healing.

As I continued my journey in oncology, I witnessed countless struggles, especially for women who had undergone mastectomies. Back then, mastectomies were often performed by general surgeons who removed the cancer but left behind scars that were more than just physical. These women had faced death and survived cancer, but they were left feeling incomplete, their bodies altered in ways that left deep emotional wounds. I remember one woman, her eyes hollow with despair, whispering to me, "I survived, but I don't feel whole anymore." Her words haunted me. I knew I had to do something to be part of a change that addressed not just the body but the soul.

One of the moments that solidified my path was when I was working with a young mother struggling to breastfeed. I noticed a small dimple on her breast, which seemed out of place. I alerted the doctor, but he brushed me off, questioning why I was looking at her breast so closely. I felt a familiar anger rising, but I stood my ground. I insisted that something was wrong, and my instincts proved correct. She had breast cancer—she was only in her twenties. It was a gut-wrenching realization, but it also reinforced what I had always known deep down: that every detail, every observation mattered. I learned that my voice and instincts mattered, even if others didn't see it at first.

Over time, my role transformed. I was no longer just a nurse; I became an oncology navigator, guiding patients through the overwhelming maze of diagnoses, treatments, and the emotional battles that followed. But the road wasn't easy. Early in my career, I was often dismissed and seen as "just a nurse." We were expected to give up our chairs when physicians entered the room, our voices silenced by a hierarchy that didn't recognize the value of our insights. But I knew my worth. I knew that nurses were the ones who spent the most time with patients, who heard their fears and held their hands in the darkest moments. We were the ones who stood by their side when everyone else had gone home.

And so, I fought to be heard. I advocated for my patients, their dignity, and their right to be seen and heard. I learned that being an oncology navigator meant more than understanding the medical side of cancer. It meant understanding each person's journey's cultural, emotional, and spiritual aspects. I worked with women from diverse backgrounds, each bringing their own stories, fears, and hopes. I learned that health equity wasn't just a concept but a responsibility. It meant meeting people where they were, honoring their cultural beliefs, and helping them navigate the system in a way that respected their values.

When I look back on my journey, I am overwhelmed with gratitude for the lives I've touched and the lessons they taught me. I think of Miss Daisy and how her strength ignited a fire in me to become more than just a nurse. I remember the young mother whose life was saved because I refused to be silent. I've seen the inequities in healthcare up close, and I've made it my mission to be a voice for those who often feel voiceless.

For me, nursing is not just a profession—it's a calling, a ministry. It's about being there for people in their most vulnerable moments, offering them hope when they feel hopeless, and helping them find the strength to keep going. I tell my patients that cancer is not a sprint; it's a marathon, and my job is to walk alongside them, one step at a time, ensuring they have the information, support, and care they need to make the best decisions for themselves.

As I look to the future, I hope we can continue to push for health equity in all aspects of oncology care. I want every patient to feel empowered, to know that they are not alone and that there are people like me ready to guide them through the most challenging times of their lives. My greatest accomplishment isn't the awards or recognition—it's the knowledge that I have helped people like Miss Daisy, that I have stood by my patients when they needed it most, and that I have made a difference in some small way.

Cancer is a battle, but it's not one that anyone should have to fight alone. I want survivors to know that there is hope, that there is strength in advocacy, and their voices matter. Together, we can navigate this journey, one step at a time, with courage, compassion, and an unyielding belief in the power of human connection.

Major Takeaways for Other Cancer Survivors:

1. **Advocacy and Empowerment:** Be proactive in your healthcare, ask questions, and make informed decisions.
2. **The Role of a Navigator:** Utilize healthcare navigators to help guide you through treatment complexities.
3. **Building a Support System:** Rely on a network of medical professionals, family, and community resources.
4. **Cultural Sensitivity and Health Equity:** Seek healthcare providers who respect and align with your cultural values.
5. **Journey, not a Race:** View cancer as a journey, taking it one step at a time.

CLEARING THE CLUTTER

REFLECTIONS

SPIRITUAL DECLUTTERING THROUGH THE ART OF STORYTELLING

The Importance of Spiritual Decluttering Through the Art of Storytelling for Cancer Survivors

Spiritual decluttering is a transformative process that can bring clarity, peace, and a renewed sense of purpose, especially for those facing the profound challenges of a cancer diagnosis. By combining this practice with the art of storytelling, cancer survivors can find a powerful means of healing and self-discovery.

Steps of Spiritual Decluttering

1. **Recognize Divine Record-Keeping:** Understand that it is God, not humans, who keeps an accurate record of all our thoughts and actions, both good and bad.
2. **Embrace God's Perspective:** Accept that God has a universal understanding of your human nature and the societal context in which you were born and raised.

3. **Heavenly Judgment:** Know that God's records of our lives are intended for a heavenly court, not a human one.
4. **Accept Divine Sacrifice:** Embrace God's substitutionary death and His willingness to reward you if you accept Him as your Savior.
5. **Acknowledge and Reject Wrongdoings:** Accept your wrongdoings that partly led to God's sacrifice on the cross and reject this undesired version of yourself.
6. **Reconciliation in Christ:** Accept that you are reconciled in Christ.
7. **Certainty of Eternal Life:** Accept the certainty of eternal life and see the positive outcome of life's challenges, including a terminal illness.

THE ROLE OF STORYTELLING

Storytelling is a profound way to process and share the journey of illness. For cancer survivors, it serves several vital functions:

1. **Expression and Release:** Sharing one's story allows one to express emotions and experiences that might otherwise remain bottled up. This release can be cathartic and help alleviate emotional burdens.
2. **Connection and Empathy:** When survivors share their stories, they connect with others experiencing similar experiences. This fosters a sense of community and mutual support, crucial for emotional and spiritual well-being.

3. **Reflection and Insight:** Narrating their journey helps survivors reflect on their experiences, gaining insights into their resilience and the lessons learned along the way. This reflection is a key component of spiritual decluttering, as it helps identify what is truly important.
4. **Empowerment and Control:** Telling their story gives survivors a sense of control over their narrative. It empowers them to define their journey on their terms rather than being defined by their illness.

Applying Spiritual Decluttering Through Storytelling

Spiritual decluttering is beneficial at any stage of life but can be particularly powerful during illness. A life-threatening condition forces us to confront our mortality, stripping away the unnecessary and revealing what is most essential. For many cancer patients, illness not only changes their bodies but also reshapes their perspective on life.

Survivors can find peace and strength by recognizing divine record-keeping, embracing God's perspective, and accepting the certainty of eternal life. Storytelling becomes a tool for spiritual decluttering, helping to navigate the complexities of illness with grace and resilience.

DEVELOPING A FRAMEWORK

Definitions and outline of steps. The steps can be both iterative and progressive.

1. **Divine Record-Keeping:**
Concept: This step draws on the idea that God is the ultimate keeper of our actions, thoughts, and intentions. It emphasizes the importance of awareness of a higher authority beyond human judgment, creating a sense of accountability.
Theological Foundation: The "Book of Life" from Christian doctrine reflects God's omniscience and the records He keeps (Revelation 13:8).

2. **Embrace God's Perspective:**
Concept: This stage requires the individual to understand that God's judgment is based on a full understanding of their life, context, and societal conditions. It encourages accepting oneself in the broader narrative of divine understanding and forgiveness.
Theological Foundation: This corresponds with God's omnipotence and His compassion towards human limitations (e.g., Psalm 139).

3. **Heavenly Judgment:**
Concept: The focus here is on the understanding that life's actions are judged by divine standards rather than human standards. This introduces a transcendent dimension of morality, freeing the individual from societal pressures.
Theological Foundation: The Bible emphasizes heavenly courts and divine judgment (e.g., 2 Corinthians 5:10).

4. **Accept Divine Sacrifice:**
Concept: This stage invites an acknowledgment of Jesus's sacrifice as a substitutionary act of love, allowing the individual to experience divine grace and reward through faith.
Theological Foundation: The atonement through Jesus's death (e.g., John 3:16) reflects this deep spiritual truth.

5. **Acknowledge and Reject Wrongdoings:**
Concept: This step focuses on recognizing one's sins and flaws and rejecting the sinful self. It is an act of confession and renunciation, freeing oneself from the burden of guilt.
Theological Foundation: Confession of sins (e.g., 1 John 1:9) leads to forgiveness and purification.

6. **Reconciliation in Christ:**
Concept: Once individuals accept their reconciliation in Christ, they are no longer condemned by their past wrongdoings. This step represents spiritual healing and wholeness.
Theological Foundation: Reconciliation is a central theme in the New Testament (e.g., 2 Corinthians 5:18–19).

7. **Certainty of Eternal Life:**
Concept: Finally, the certainty of eternal life offers peace and comfort, even in the face of terminal illness or life's challenges. It helps reframe suffering as temporary in the context of eternal joy.
Theological Foundation: The promise of eternal life through faith in Christ (e.g., John 14:1–3).

Application in Illness and Life Crises:

As detailed in the stories of cancer patients within the book, **spiritual decluttering** helps individuals gain clarity in their lives during illness by identifying what truly matters—faith, relationships, and inner peace. This decluttering becomes a process of shedding societal expectations, fear of death, and guilt, leading to a spiritual and existential transformation that brings healing beyond the physical.

This spiritual framework weaves spiritual truths together, providing individuals with a structured path toward spiritual liberation and deeper peace.

To integrate evidence from the participants' essays into the **Spiritual Decluttering Framework**, we can use personal experiences to illustrate the practical application and emotional significance of each step. These real-life narratives offer keen insights into how spiritual decluttering works in moments of illness, crisis, and self-transformation.

1. **Divine Record-Keeping:**
Participant Example: In the essay by Chris Knight, his cancer diagnosis led him to reflect on his past life, asking, "Have

I been a good husband? Have I been a good father? Have I been a good friend?" This moment of deep reflection shows how facing illness brings the realization that life is being "recorded," not just by those around us but in a divine sense. Chris's journey illustrates the first step of spiritual decluttering: recognizing that God keeps a record of our lives and actions, forcing a reevaluation of priorities and past behavior.

2. **Embrace God's Perspective:**

Participant Example: David Nkoma's diagnosis of non-Hodgkin's lymphoma at 61 also pushed him to confront his mortality. He reflected on how his brothers had all passed away before the age of 55, and he began to feel that he was "living in extra time." Yet, instead of sinking into despair, he embraced the idea that his survival was part of God's plan. His acceptance of God's perspective understanding the broader context of his life and challenges, allowed him to find peace in his diagnosis. This illustrates the second step: accepting that God understands our human limitations and societal contexts.

3. **Heavenly Judgment:**

Participant Example: Tracia Williams's experience with breast cancer represents this step. She mentioned that despite being diagnosed with cancer, she never lost sight of the fact that her faith in God remained her greatest source of strength. She stated, "God is the source of my strength." Tracia's faith assured her that the true judgment of her life and actions was divine, not human. This step freed her from fear and focused her attention on her relationship with God, emphasizing that divine judgment surpasses human trials.

4. **Accept Divine Sacrifice:**

Participant Example: Ariane Navarro's story of surviving leukemia at a young age highlights the acceptance of divine sacrifice. Faced with a relapse just three months after giving birth, Ariane expressed anger and frustration at God. However, over time, she came to terms with her suffering and found the strength to focus on surviving for her family. Her experience represents the spiritual decluttering step of accepting the divine sacrifice, where the individual acknowledges God's grace through personal trials and expresses gratitude for life despite the hardship.

5. **Acknowledge and Reject Wrongdoings:**

Participant Example: Vivia Haye, after being diagnosed with aggressive breast cancer, experienced severe physical weakness and emotional exhaustion during chemotherapy. A critical turning point came when a nurse asked her, "Do you want to be a statistic, or are you going to fight?" This blunt question forced Vivia to confront her fear, weakness, and feelings of hopelessness, pushing her to reject any defeatist mentality. This illustrates the process of rejecting undesirable aspects of oneself—whether it's negativity, fear, or moral failings—and reorienting one's life toward healing and faith.

6. **Reconciliation in Christ:**

Participant Example: Ariane Navarro, despite her anger at God, eventually found reconciliation by using writing as her lifeline. She poured out her emotions, reflections, and confessions on paper, helping her make sense of her experience and accept her new reality. This process of creative expression allowed her to reconcile her suffering and faith, showing how the individual, through acceptance, finds spiritual healing in Christ. Reconciliation in Christ is about embracing the new self, healed and whole in faith.

7. **Certainty of Eternal Life:**

Participant Example: David Nkoma's battle with cancer encapsulated this step as he described his survival as "healing," not merely remission. Despite the lasting side effects, David viewed his continued existence as a divine gift and embraced each day with gratitude. This sense of hope and eternal life allowed David to see his battle with cancer as part of a greater plan. His story represents how spiritual decluttering transforms one's view of life's challenges into moments of existential clarity and hope.

Conclusion: Spiritual Decluttering in Illness

The common thread across the participants' experiences is that illness stripped away the unnecessary distractions and clarified what matters most—faith, relationships, and personal meaning. In each case, the author puts forward that spiritual decluttering allowed them to face mortality, reconcile their lives, and embrace their spiritual identities. The framework of spiritual decluttering, grounded in faith, became a path to peace amidst life's most difficult challenges.

SPIRITUAL DECLUTTERING WORKSHEET

This worksheet is designed to help you engage in the process of **Spiritual Decluttering**, guiding you through personal reflection and transformative exercises based on the experiences of cancer survivors who found peace, clarity, and meaning through their journeys. The goal is to declutter your spirit by acknowledging your past, embracing your faith, and aligning your life with your highest purpose.

Part 1: Recognizing Divine Record-Keeping:

Reflection Prompt: Think about your life's journey. Reflect on both your successes and your mistakes. Consider how you believe your life is "recorded" by a higher power.

1. Write down key moments that define your spiritual and personal journey (both positive and negative):

Key moments of success:
_____
_____
_____

Key mistakes/failures:
_____
_____
_____
_____

Guided Exercise: Consider what Chris Knight asked during his cancer journey: "Have I been a good [spouse, parent, friend]?" Write down three questions you can ask yourself to understand better how your actions are being "recorded."

1. _____
2. _____
3. _____

SPIRITUAL DECLUTTERING WORKSHEET

Part 2: Embracing God's Perspective:

Reflection Prompt: God understands your personal context—where you came from, the challenges you've faced, and your unique experiences.

1. What are some societal or cultural factors that have shaped you? How do you think God views these influences in your life?

   _____
   _____
   _____
   _____

2. List three aspects of your life that you believe are understood from a divine perspective:

   _____
   _____
   _____

Guided Exercise: David Nkoma embraced his journey with faith despite his cancer diagnosis. Try to accept your challenges in the same way. Write a letter to yourself from God's perspective, reminding you of your strengths and unique qualities.

   _____
   _____
   _____
   _____

Part 3: Understanding Heavenly Judgment:

Reflection Prompt: Know that your actions are judged by a heavenly court, not a human one. Reflect on how this changes your perspective on what truly matters.

1. What human judgments or societal pressures are you currently facing? How can you release yourself from these judgments by focusing on divine judgment?

   _____
   _____
   _____
   _____

2. Write down three areas where you need to shift your focus from human approval to divine approval:

   _____
   _____
   _____

Guided Exercise: Imagine standing in front of God's judgment. List three things you think matter most to Him when considering your life.

1. _____
2. _____
3. _____

SPIRITUAL DECLUTTERING WORKSHEET

Part 4: Accepting Divine Sacrifice:

Reflection Prompt: Reflect on the idea of divine sacrifice—God's willingness to offer grace and salvation. How do you embrace that sacrifice in your life?

1. What sacrifices have you accepted as part of your spiritual journey (such as letting go of past hurts or embracing forgiveness)?

   _____
   _____
   _____
   _____

2. Write about a time when you experienced grace, even when you felt undeserving:

   _____
   _____
   _____
   _____

Guided Exercise: Dr. Vivia Haye found grace in survival. Spend a few minutes meditating on gratitude, focusing on moments when you felt a sense of divine protection. Write down three things you are grateful for in your spiritual journey:

1. _____
2. _____
3. _____

Part 5: Acknowledging and Rejecting Wrongdoings:

Reflection Prompt: Acknowledge your mistakes and wrongdoings. This step is about recognizing the version of yourself that you no longer wish to carry forward.

1. List three behaviors or attitudes that no longer serve you and that you are ready to reject:

1. _____
2. _____
3. _____

Guided Exercise: Ariane's acknowledgment of her struggles, including her overdoses and moments of mental health crises, aligns with this step of spiritual decluttering. She does not shy away from accepting her wrongdoings, even when faced with judgment from others who cannot understand her battle with depression and addiction. Her openness about these moments and her recognition that they were part of a larger emotional response to her illness allows her to reject the darker version of herself that almost gave in to despair.

Part 6: Reconciliation in Christ:

Reflection Prompt: Reconciliation means accepting that you are forgiven and whole in Christ (or within your faith). How does this concept bring healing and peace to you?

1. What does reconciliation mean to you? How have you experienced it in your life?

   _____
   _____
   _____

2. Write down a situation where you reconciled with someone (or yourself) and felt a sense of peace afterward:

   _____
   _____
   _____

Guided Exercise: Like Ariane Navarro, try using writing as a form of reconciliation. Write a letter to your past self, expressing forgiveness and gratitude for the lessons learned.

Part 7: Certainty of Eternal Life:

Reflection Prompt: Reflect on the certainty of eternal life and how it changes your perspective on your challenges and future.

1. How does the belief in eternal life or spiritual continuity comfort you in times of distress?

   _____
   _____
   _____

2. Write about how you can face life's challenges, including illness, with the knowledge that eternal life is guaranteed:

   _____
   _____
   _____

Guided Exercise: David Nkoma found strength in the idea that he was living in "extra time" beyond the years his brothers had lived. Write a declaration about how you will live each day with purpose and meaning, focusing on what matters most to you.

Closing Reflection:

After completing this worksheet, take a moment to reflect on how the process of spiritual decluttering has helped you gain clarity. How has confronting your past, embracing God's perspective, and accepting divine judgment helped you reorder your priorities?

Final Thought:

Just as cancer survivors find clarity through illness, spiritual decluttering helps you confront what truly matters in life. Use this space to write any lingering thoughts, prayers, or intentions that have surfaced through this exercise:

CONTACTING THE AUTHOR FOR SEMINARS, CONFERENCES, AND LECTURES

If the concept of spiritual decluttering inspires you through storytelling and you would like to delve deeper into this transformative practice, I invite you to connect with me, Throy Campbell, the founder of Cultivating Health Narratives. I am passionate about sharing these insights and facilitating meaningful conversations through seminars, conferences, and lectures.

To host an event or learn more about my work, please visit CultivatingHealthNarratives.com. On the website, you will find additional resources, information about upcoming events, and ways to get in touch.

Whether you are a cancer survivor, healthcare professional, or someone seeking personal growth, these sessions are designed to provide valuable tools and perspectives. Together, we can explore the art of spiritual decluttering and its profound impact on our lives.

I look forward to connecting and sharing this journey with you.

Warm regards,
Throy Campbell Founder, Cultivating Health Narratives

ENDNOTES

1. J.S. Beck, *Cognitive Behavior Therapy: Basics and Beyond*, 2nd Ed. (New York: Guilford Press, 2020).

2. M.E.P. Seligman, *Authentic Happiness: Using the New Positive Psychology to Realize Your Potential for Lasting Fulfillment.* (New York: Free Press, 2002).

    C.R. Rogers, *On Becoming a Person: A Therapist's View of Psychotherapy.* (Boston: Houghton Mifflin, 1961).

    I.D. Yalom, *Existential Psychotherapy.* (New York: Basic Books, 1980).

    V.E. Frankl, *Man's Search for Meaning.* (Boston: Beacon Press, 1959).

    K.D. Neff, *Self-Compassion: The Proven Power of Being Kind to Yourself.* (New York: William Morrow, 2011).

MORE BY THROY CAMPBELL

From humble beginnings in Jamaica to achieving academic success in the United States, this memoir tells the powerful story of a life shaped by faith, perseverance, and the enduring love of family. Throy Campbell, PhD, reflects on the profound influence of his mother's unwavering faith and countless sacrifices, which paved the way for his success.

Through personal stories, Throy shares the challenges he faced as an international student, the complexities of navigating a career in academia, and his commitment to mentoring underrepresented students. With a focus on the values of faith, determination, and service, the memoir offers encouragement to those striving for success with limited resources and reminds readers that with God, all things are possible.

At its heart, the memoir is a testament to the power of faith and the belief that, no matter where you start, you can achieve greatness by trusting in God's plan.

www.ingramcontent.com/pod-product-compliance
Lightning Source LLC
Chambersburg PA
CBHW060656100426
42734CB00047B/1928